THE ENTREPRENEUR'S DESK

A STEP-BY-STEP PRACTICAL GUIDE TO ACCOUNTING FOR SME SUCCESS

AF486209

CA. GAURAV AGRAWAL

Copyright © CA. Gaurav Agrawal 2024
All Rights Reserved.

ISBN
Paperback 979-8-89446-669-9
Hardcase 979-8-89475-383-6

Disclaimer

The information provided in this book is intended for general informational purposes only and should not be construed as professional advice. While every effort has been made to ensure the accuracy and completeness of the information presented, the author and publisher make no representations or warranties of any kind, express or implied, about the completeness, accuracy, reliability, suitability, or availability with respect to the content contained herein for any purpose.

Readers are advised to consult with a qualified professional accountant before implementing any of the strategies, tips, techniques, or suggestions discussed in this book. The author and publisher disclaim any liability for any loss or damage arising directly or indirectly from the use of the information provided.

Furthermore, the views expressed in this book are solely those of the author(s) and do not necessarily reflect the views of any organizations mentioned herein. Any reference to specific products, services, companies, or organizations does not imply endorsement or recommendation by the author or publisher.

Dedication

In loving memory of my father, Shri Gopal Ji Agrawal, whose enduring values continue to inspire me.

To my mother, Manju Agrawal, whose resilience and love have been a guiding light.

To my wife, Priya Agrawal, whose steadfast support and encouragement have made this endeavor possible.

And to my children, Gauri and Garv, whose endless curiosity inspires me to share knowledge and experiences.

CONTENTS

ABOUT THE AUTHOR

CA. Gaurav Agrawal is a distinguished Chartered Accountant with a robust professional background. He has been a member of the Institute of Chartered Accountants of India (ICAI) since 2004 and ascended to the status of Fellow Member in 2009. His expertise is further underscored by his qualification as an Insolvency Professional with the Insolvency and Bankruptcy Board of India since 2018.

In his relentless pursuit of excellence, CA. Agrawal has augmented his professional credentials with various specialized certification courses offered by the ICAI. These include:

- Diploma in Information System Audit

- Certificate Course on GST

- Certificate Course on Concurrent Audit of Banks

- Certificate Course on Forensic Audit & Fraud Prevention

- Certificate Course on Preparation of Appeals, Drafting of Deed & Documents, and Representation before Appellate Authorities and Statutory Bodies

CA. Gaurav Agrawal areas of keen interest encompass Accounting, Auditing, Project Financing, and assisting in Investment & Employment Promotion Schemes from both Central and State governments tailored for SMEs. His vast knowledge and experience make him a sought-after speaker on numerous platforms where he addresses a range of topics related to Accounts Management, business development, and support available to SME entrepreneurs.

Beyond his professional commitments, CA. Gaurav Agrawal is deeply passionate about empowering SMEs through education and practical support. He has been instrumental in guiding small and medium enterprises towards sustainable growth by leveraging various government schemes and financial tools. His dedication to fostering a robust SME ecosystem is reflected in his contributions as an author, where he distils complex financial concepts into accessible knowledge for budding entrepreneurs and established business owners alike.

FOREWORD – CA. KAMAL GARG

In the dynamic and challenging landscape of modern business, small and medium enterprises (SMEs) serve as the backbone of economic growth and innovation. However, the path to success for SME entrepreneurs is fraught with numerous challenges, not least of which is the need for robust and accurate accounting practices. It is within this context that **"The Entrepreneur's Desk: A Step by Step Practical Guide to Accounting for SME Success"** by CA. Gaurav Agrawal emerges as an invaluable resource.

As a fellow Chartered Accountant, I have witnessed firsthand the complexities that entrepreneurs face when managing their financial affairs. The ability to maintain clear, precise, and effective accounting records is not merely a regulatory requirement but a critical component of sustainable business growth and development. CA Gaurav Agrawal, with his extensive experience and deep understanding of the subject, has crafted a guide that demystifies accounting principles and makes them accessible to all.

This book stands out for its practical approach, which is tailored specifically to the needs of SMEs. It breaks down intricate accounting concepts into straightforward, actionable steps that entrepreneurs can easily implement. From understanding the basics of financial statements to navigating the nuances of Financial Analysis Interpretation, this handbook provides comprehensive insights that empower business owners to take control of their financial health.

CA Gaurav Agrawal's clear and concise writing style, combined with real-world examples and practical tips, ensures that readers can quickly grasp and apply the information. In today's fast-paced business environment, the ability to make informed financial decisions is crucial. **"The Entrepreneur's Desk: A Step by Step Practical Guide to Accounting for SME Success"** equips SME entrepreneurs with the knowledge and confidence needed to manage their finances effectively, paving the way for long-term success.

I commend CA. Gaurav Agrawal for his dedication to simplifying the complexities of accounting and for his contribution to the entrepreneurial community. It is with great pleasure that I write this foreword and wholeheartedly recommend this book to all SME entrepreneurs striving for excellence in their financial management.

CA. Kamal Garg

BEST WISHES – DR. AJAY SHESH

I have known CA Gaurav Agrawal for more than five years now and have been in amazement of his domain knowledge and advisory expertise. His added ability as a trainer/speaker and ability to explain complex accounting concepts to entrepreneurs in a simple manner is a rare virtue found in few. Over the years I have observed a deep desire in him to add value to his clients and students for their wholesome business and personal growth - apart from his professional job as a Chartered Accountant. Hence it came as a pleasant surprise when yet another feather in his cap - that of an author was revealed to me. As I went through the manuscript of this book **"The Entrepreneur's Desk: A Step by Step Practical Guide to Accounting for SME Success"** the layout of topics and the contents therein were a revelation to me.

He begins this book not by direct advisory pattern but touching the deep pain points of today's SME Entrepreneur. I have always believed that Mindset plays 80% role in any successful Business Growth initiative. CA Gaurav has done just that by talking about the mindset of accounting and the Fundamental Golden Rules that entrepreneurs must follow.

Dear Reader, by the time you reach the second half of the book, you will become ready to absorb the slightly complex and numerical aspects of accounting. To make this even easier - lot of practical examples have been included for the reader to digest the content. MCQs at the end will help you revise the important facts. You will get the full taste of this book only when you read it patiently and with focus. This is not a book to be read once and kept away. I would strongly advise you to use this book as a reference resource, and use the specific chapters to gain insight and solutions for specific issues you face in Business.

CA Gaurav Agrawal has created a valuable publication by finding out time from his very busy schedule. We entrepreneurs must appreciate and thank him from the bottom of our hearts. I have always believed that CA Gaurav Agrawal deserves a national level of acclaim for his expertise and contributions. With the authorship this Book **"The Entrepreneur's Desk: A Step by Step Practical Guide to Accounting for SME Success"** a step in this direction has been taken. I wish all the best to this book for reaching a countrywide audience and create waves all over the country.

As the Founder and Chief Mentor of "Life Champions Ecosystem", India's premier Entrepreneur Training Platform, I express my best wishes and gratitude to you, the reader, for picking up this book.

DR AJAY SHESH
MBBS MD MBA MPhil, PhD
Founder - Life Champions Ecosystem

PREFACE

India's growth is closely tied to the rise of Micro, Small & Medium Enterprises (MSMEs), which are important in every state, union territory, and district. MSMEs are the backbone of the supply chain and provide many jobs in society. They meet local market needs while also aiming to expand globally. Entrepreneurs running these MSMEs are the nation's hidden heroes, building a strong economic foundation. Just as soldiers defend our borders, these entrepreneurs protect and grow our economy.

No large company can succeed without first being an MSME. The path to creating a big, sustainable business starts with managing an MSME. In these smaller ventures, entrepreneurs develop essential skills, systems, and strong teams.

Think about the local shops that have been around for years, with owners working hard from morning to night. These self-employed people build trust and reliability in their communities. Their businesses, supported by other MSMEs like wholesalers, distributors, and manufacturers, form a strong supply chain. Even large manufacturers rely on MSMEs for goods and services, showing how important MSMEs are to the entire economy.

In India, with a population of 1.41 billion, meeting the needs of such a vast populace efficiently and economically requires a decentralized structure of goods and services. Strengthening MSMEs is paramount to ensuring the ecosystem functions effectively, serving the local areas and, by extension, the nation.

In today's dynamic business environment, small and medium-sized entrepreneurs (SMEs) often grapple with the challenge of maintaining efficient and effective accounting systems. While many SME owners and managers excel in their respective fields, they often lack formal accounting knowledge. This book aims to bridge that gap, offering practical guidance on establishing and managing an accounting system tailored specifically for SMEs.

"The Entrepreneur's Desk" symbolizes a place of comfort and control, where every SME entrepreneur can feel empowered to manage their business finances with confidence. Just as a desk is a central workspace for executives, this book provides the essential tools and knowledge for SME entrepreneurs to oversee their accounting practices seamlessly, enabling them to focus on growth and innovation.

Having navigated these challenges firsthand, I understand the crucial role a robust accounting framework plays in the success and sustainability of any business venture. This book is a product of my experiences and the insights gained from interacting with numerous entrepreneurs facing similar hurdles.

The objective of this book is not merely to explain accounting principles but to provide a step-by-step roadmap for SME entrepreneurs unfamiliar with accounting practices. It addresses the fundamental need for clear and accurate financial record-keeping, highlighting common pitfalls and offering strategies to overcome them. By demystifying accounting processes and terminology, we empower entrepreneurs to manage their finances confidently and make informed business decisions.

Throughout these pages, readers will find practical tips and tricks that can be immediately implemented, whether setting up initial accounting procedures or streamlining existing systems. We emphasize simplicity and clarity, recognizing that complex accounting methods can be daunting for those new to the field.

I am indebted to Dr. Ajay Shesh, my mentor, whose encouragement and guidance were instrumental in bringing this project to fruition. His expertise and passion for entrepreneurship have enriched this book immeasurably.

I extend my deepest gratitude to Prof. Dr. Rishi Acharya for his invaluable guidance in structuring the layout and assisting with the publication of this book. A heartfelt thank you to CA N. L. Gupta, who has always been a guiding light.

I would also like to express my sincere appreciation to my brother-in-law, CA. Ashish Agrawal. As a veteran in his field and an accomplished author of numerous books, his insights and advice have been immensely helpful.

May this book serve as a beacon for entrepreneurs, guiding them through the complexities of accounting and financial management.

Readers may send their queries and suggestions to my email: gaurav81@gmail.com.

COMMON ACCOUNTING PROBLEMS FOR SMEs

Small and medium-sized enterprises (SMEs) often face a variety of accounting challenges that can impact their financial health and operational efficiency. Here are some common accounting issues faced by SMEs:

1. **Mindset Issue:**

   o Small and medium-sized enterprise (SME) entrepreneurs often excel in sales, marketing, and product development but lack a background in accounting, leading to avoidance of financial statements. This gap hinders their understanding of their company's financial health, affecting decision-making and strategic planning.

- SME entrepreneurs frequently view accounting and financial reporting compliances as cost centres rather than tools for tracking and achieving business goals. They show a lack of interest in learning basic accounting, viewing it as tedious and non-essential compared to their focus on sales, marketing, and product development. This reluctance leads to over-reliance on accountants, resulting in missed insights from financial statements crucial for informed decision-making and business sustainability.

2. Limited Financial Expertise:

- SMEs often lack the resources to hire experienced accounting professionals. As a result, business owners or untrained staff handle accounting tasks, leading to potential errors and inefficiencies.

- Limited financial expertise can also affect strategic financial planning and analysis.

3. Inventory Management:

- Poor inventory management can lead to issues such as overstocking, stockouts, and increased holding costs.

- Inaccurate inventory records can distort financial statements and lead to cash flow problems.

4. Debt Management:

- Managing debt effectively is crucial for maintaining financial health. SMEs often face challenges in balancing debt levels, ensuring timely repayments, and managing interest expenses.

- Poor debt management can lead to financial strain and affect creditworthiness.

5. Bookkeeping Errors:

- Inaccurate or incomplete bookkeeping can lead to significant financial discrepancies. Common errors include incorrect data entry, failure to record transactions, and misclassification of expenses.

o These errors can distort financial statements, leading to poor decision-making and potential compliance issues.

6. **Cash Flow Management:**

o SMEs often struggle with maintaining a steady cash flow. Late payments from customers, high inventory levels, and unexpected expenses can cause cash flow problems.

o Inadequate cash flow forecasting and planning can lead to liquidity issues, affecting the ability to meet short-term obligations.

7. **Compliance and Regulatory Requirements:**

o Keeping up with constantly changing tax laws, regulations, and reporting standards can be challenging for SMEs.

o Failure to comply with these requirements can result in fines, penalties, and legal issues.

8. **Technology Integration:**

o Many SMEs struggle with integrating accounting software and other technologies to streamline their accounting processes.

o Manual accounting processes can be time-consuming and prone to errors, while the lack of proper technology can hinder efficient financial management.

9. **Cost Control:**

o Managing and controlling costs is a critical issue for SMEs. Without proper accounting practices, it can be challenging to track expenses, manage budgets, and identify cost-saving opportunities.

o Overspending or unmonitored expenses can erode profit margins and financial stability.

10. Financial Reporting:

- Producing accurate and timely financial reports is essential for decision-making and stakeholder communication. SMEs often struggle with generating reliable financial reports due to inadequate accounting systems and processes.

- Inaccurate financial reporting can lead to poor business decisions and affect investor confidence.

11. Taxation Issues:

- Navigating the complexities of tax regulations, deductions, and filings can be overwhelming for SMEs.

- Incorrect tax filings can result in penalties, interest charges, and audits from tax authorities.

We have tried to address on each issue through this Book to navigate the challenges faced by the SME Entrepreneur in accounting

* * *

Chapter Challenge: Test Your Understanding with MCQs

1. **What is a common mindset issue among SME entrepreneurs regarding accounting?**

    (A) SMEs prioritize accounting over sales and marketing.

    (B) SME entrepreneurs often lack interest in learning basic accounting.

    (C) SMEs view accounting as the most crucial aspect of business management.

    (D) SMEs hire experienced accounting professionals to handle all financial tasks.

2. What is a consequence of limited financial expertise in SMEs?

(A) Improved strategic financial planning

(B) Efficient management of accounting tasks

(C) Potential errors and inefficiencies in accounting

(D) Increased profitability

3. What problem can arise from poor inventory management in SMEs?

(A) Decreased holding costs

(B) Efficient cash flow management

(C) Stockouts and increased holding costs

(D) Accurate financial reporting

4. Why is effective debt management crucial for SMEs?

(A) It doesn't affect financial health.

(B) It helps maintain creditworthiness and financial stability.

(C) It leads to increased debt levels.

(D) It results in reduced interest expenses.

5. What can inaccurate bookkeeping lead to in SMEs?

(A) Improved decision-making

(B) Correct financial statements

(C) Significant financial discrepancies

(D) Compliance with regulatory requirements

Answers

1.(B),   2.(C),   3.(C),   4.(B),   5.(C)

FIRST THINGS FIRST: CULTIVATING THE RIGHT MINDSET FOR MANAGING ACCOUNTS

2.1   Why It Should Be a Priority for Sme Entrepreneurs

In the dynamic landscape of small and medium enterprises (SMEs), where entrepreneurs often wear multiple hats, the accounting department frequently faces unique challenges that can hinder business growth and efficiency. While handling various facets of business management such as **administration, operations, sales, marketing, human resources, and research and development**, accounting sometimes gets relegated to the background, leading to significant mindset issues. Addressing these mindset issues is crucial for SMEs to maintain financial health and ensure long-term success.

2.2   The Importance of Accounting in SMEs

Accounting is the backbone of any business, providing critical insights into financial health, aiding in decision-making, and ensuring compliance with legal requirements. For SMEs, accurate and timely accounting is vital for managing cash flow, securing financing, and planning for growth. Despite its importance, many SMEs struggle with establishing an effective accounting department, primarily due to mindset issues that stem from misconceptions, lack of expertise, and underestimation of its value.

2.3 Common Mindset Issues in the Accounting Department

1. **Perception of Accounting as a Cost Centre**: Many SME entrepreneurs view accounting merely as a necessary expense rather than a strategic function. This perception leads to minimal investment in accounting resources, technology, and skilled personnel. Consequently, the accounting department operates in a reactive rather than proactive manner, focusing on basic compliance and bookkeeping instead of strategic financial planning and analysis.

2. **Underestimation of Accounting Complexity**: SME owners often underestimate the complexity of accounting tasks, assuming that basic bookkeeping suffices for their needs. This mindset can result in overlooking critical aspects such as financial forecasting, budgeting, tax planning, and internal controls. Without these functions, SMEs are vulnerable to financial mismanagement, cash flow issues, and missed growth opportunities.

3. **Lack of Financial Literacy**: Many SME entrepreneurs possess limited financial literacy, leading to a lack of appreciation for detailed financial reports and analysis. This gap in understanding can result in poor financial decision-making and an inability to leverage accounting insights for strategic planning. Entrepreneurs may also struggle to communicate effectively with accountants, further diminishing the potential impact of the accounting function.

4. **Resistance to Technology Adoption**: In an era where accounting software and automation tools can significantly enhance efficiency, some SMEs remain resistant to adopting new technologies. This resistance often stems from a mindset rooted in tradition and fear of change. Without leveraging technology, SMEs miss out on streamlined processes, real-time financial data, and analytical tools that can drive better business decisions.

5. **Reactive Approach to Financial Management**: SMEs often adopt a reactive approach to financial management, addressing issues as they arise rather than planning proactively. This mindset can

lead to crises such as cash flow shortages, unexpected tax liabilities, and unanticipated expenses. A proactive accounting department, on the other hand, can anticipate and mitigate financial risks, ensuring smoother operations and stability.

2.4 The Right Mindset to Manage the Accounting Department in SMEs

To effectively manage the accounting department in SMEs, adopting the right mindset is crucial. This involves recognizing the strategic value of accounting, fostering a culture of financial literacy, investing in technology, and promoting proactive financial management. Below are key elements of the right mindset and how to implement them, accompanied by practical examples.

1. **Viewing Accounting as a Strategic Partner:**

   o **Mindset Shift:** Understand that accounting is not just a back-office function but a strategic partner that provides valuable insights for decision-making and business growth.

   o **Practical Example:** An SME in the retail sector can leverage accounting data to identify the most profitable product lines and the best times for promotions. By analyzing sales trends, cost structures, and profit margins, the accounting team can provide recommendations on inventory management and pricing strategies, directly impacting profitability.

2. Prioritizing Financial Literacy

- o **Mindset Shift:** Encourage continuous learning and development in financial management among all key personnel, not just the accounting team.

- o **Practical Example:** A tech startup organizes monthly financial literacy workshops for its staff, focusing on interpreting financial statements, understanding cash flow management, and budgeting. This empowers the entire team to make informed decisions, align their actions with financial goals, and communicate effectively with the accounting department.

3. Investing in Technology and Automation

- o **Mindset Shift:** Embrace modern accounting software and automation tools to enhance efficiency, accuracy, and real-time financial reporting.

- o **Practical Example:** An SME in the manufacturing industry invests in an integrated ERP (Enterprise Resource Planning) system that includes advanced accounting modules. This system automates routine tasks like invoicing, payroll, and financial reporting, freeing up the accounting team to focus on analysis and strategic planning. The real-time data provided by the ERP system allows for better cash flow management and timely financial insights.

4. Promoting Proactive Financial Management

- o **Mindset Shift:** Shift from reactive to proactive financial management, with regular forecasting, budgeting, and risk assessments.

- o **Practical Example:** A hospitality business, such as a chain of boutique hotels, holds quarterly financial planning meetings where the accounting team presents forecasts and budgets for the upcoming period. By reviewing past performance and adjusting for seasonal variations, the business can plan for peak seasons, manage expenses during off-peak times, and make informed decisions about marketing and staffing.

5. **Integrating Accounting into Strategic Planning**

  o **Mindset Shift:** Ensure that accounting is an integral part of the strategic planning process, influencing decisions on investments, expansions, and other major initiatives.

  o **Practical Example:** An SME in the food and beverage industry considering opening a new outlet involves the accounting team from the outset. The accountants provide a detailed financial feasibility study, including cost projections, break-even analysis, and funding requirements. This input helps the management team make an informed decision about the expansion, ensuring financial sustainability.

2.5 Implementing the Right Mindset

To successfully implement these mindset shifts, SMEs can take the following steps:

- **Leadership Commitment:** Leadership must demonstrate a commitment to learning, valuing, and integrating the accounting function. This can be achieved by understanding and writing standard operating procedures (SOPs) for each step of the accounting systems and processes.

- **Regular Reviews:** Creating one-time SOPs is not a long-term solution. Regular reviews and updates are essential for effectively automating the accounting system within the organization. This ensures that financial goals are aligned with business objectives and that any issues are addressed proactively.

- **Continuous Training:** Regularly participate in and organize training sessions and workshops on accounting processes and financial management for the team. Stay updated with new concepts and rules as advised by the government and plan carefully. This helps build a culture of financial awareness and literacy across the organization.

- **Technology Adoption:** Allocate a budget for modern accounting software and tools. Provide training to ensure the team can effectively use these technologies to streamline processes and enhance productivity.

- **Clear Communication Channels:** Establish clear communication channels between management, the accounting department, and other departments. This fosters collaboration and ensures that financial considerations are integrated into all aspects of the business.

By adopting this right mindset, SMEs can transform their accounting departments into strategic assets that drive growth, enhance efficiency, and ensure long-term financial stability. To start with first understand the **Fundamentals of Accounting**

* * *

Chapter Challenge: Test Your Understanding with MCQs

1. **Why should SME entrepreneurs prioritize cultivating the right mindset for managing accounts?**

   (A) To reduce the cost of accounting services

   (B) To ensure compliance with tax laws only

   (C) To maintain financial health and ensure long-term success

   (D) To minimize the need for external financial advisors

2. **What is a common misconception about accounting in SMEs?**

   (A) Accounting is seen as a strategic function

   (B) Accounting is viewed as a cost centre

   (C) Accounting complexity is overestimated

   (D) Financial literacy is widely appreciated

3. **How can SMEs address the issue of underestimation of accounting complexity?**

    (A) By relying solely on basic bookkeeping

    (B) By ignoring financial forecasting and budgeting

    (C) By recognizing the need for financial forecasting, budgeting, tax planning, and internal controls

    (D) By avoiding investment in skilled personnel

4. **What is a recommended approach to promote proactive financial management in SMEs?**

    (A) Addressing financial issues as they arise

    (B) Holding quarterly financial planning meetings with regular forecasting and budgeting

    (C) Focusing solely on basic compliance and bookkeeping

    (D) Avoiding technology adoption in accounting

5. **Which practical example illustrates the integration of accounting into strategic planning in SMEs?**

    (A) Organizing monthly financial literacy workshops for staff

    (B) Investing in an ERP system that includes advanced accounting modules

    (C) Involving the accounting team in the decision-making process for opening a new outlet

    (D) Viewing accounting as a necessary expense

Answers:

1.(C),　　2.(B),　　3.(C),　　4 (B),　　5.(C)

FUNDAMENTALS OF ACCOUNTING

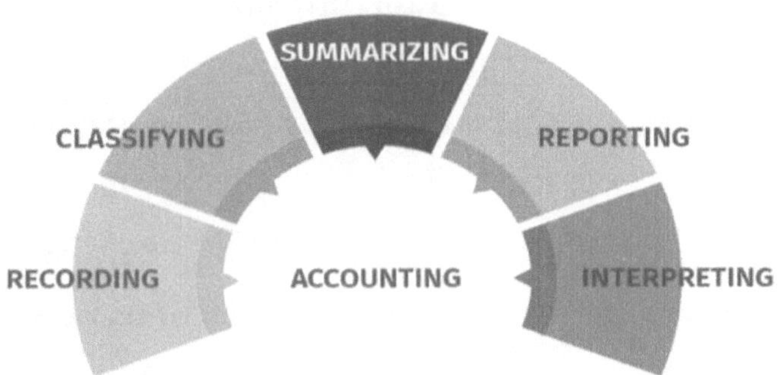

The fundamentals of accounting for encompass several key processes: recording, classifying, summarizing, reporting, and interpreting financial information. Let's break down each of these elements in detail:

1. **Recording:**

    Recording involves the systematic documentation of financial transactions as they occur within the business. This process captures all relevant information about each transaction, including the date, amount, parties involved, and nature of the transaction. Commonly used documents for recording transactions include invoices, receipts, bank statements, and purchase orders.

    Methods of Recording:

    o   Manual Recording: Using physical journals or ledgers to record transactions.

    o   Electronic Recording: Utilizing accounting software to input and store transaction data.

2. Classifying:

Classifying refers to categorizing recorded transactions into specific accounts based on their nature (e.g., revenue, expenses, assets, liabilities, equity). This step involves assigning appropriate account codes or categories to each transaction, ensuring accuracy and consistency in financial reporting.

Common Account Categories:

- o Assets: Tangible (e.g., cash, inventory) and intangible assets (e.g., patents, goodwill).

- o Liabilities: Debts and obligations owed by the business (e.g., loans, accounts payable).

- o Equity: Owner's investment and retained earnings.

- o Revenue: Income generated from sales or services.

- o Expenses: Costs incurred in the course of business operations (e.g., salaries, rent).

3. Summarising:

Summarising involves compiling classified transactions into financial statements, such as the income statement, balance sheet, and cash flow statement. This step aggregates financial data over specific periods (e.g., monthly, quarterly, annually) to provide a clear overview of the business's financial performance and position.

Key Financial Statements:

- o Income Statement (Profit and Loss Statement): Summarises revenues and expenses to determine net income or loss.

- o Balance Sheet: Presents assets, liabilities, and equity at a specific point in time, reflecting the business's financial position.

- o Cash Flow Statement: Tracks cash inflows and outflows during a specified period, highlighting sources and uses of cash.

4. Reporting:

Reporting involves preparing and distributing financial statements to stakeholders, such as business owners, investors, creditors, and regulatory authorities. Financial reports provide valuable insights into the SME's financial health, performance, and potential risks.

Types of Reports:

- o Internal Reports: Used for management decision-making and performance evaluation.

- o External Reports: Shared with external parties, including investors, lenders, and government agencies.

5. Interpreting:

Interpreting financial information is the process of analyzing and deriving meaningful insights from financial reports. This step helps stakeholders understand the implications of financial data and make informed decisions regarding the business's operations, investments, and future strategies.

Key Aspects of Interpretation:

- o Financial Ratios: Calculations (e.g., profitability ratios, liquidity ratios) used to assess financial performance and stability.

- o Trend Analysis: Examining patterns and changes in financial data over time to identify strengths, weaknesses, and emerging opportunities.

As mentioned above, Entrepreneurs need to **classify** accounting transactions under various categories to effectively summarize, report & Interpret the Financial Statement. Understanding the **Golden Rules of Accounting** is key to grasping the basic concept of classification.

* * *

Chapter Challenge: Test Your Understanding with MCQs

1. **Which of the following is NOT a common document used for recording transactions?**

   (A) Invoice

   (B) Receipt

   (C) Tax Return

   (D) Bank Statement

2. **What is the primary purpose of classifying transactions in accounting?**

   (A) To record each transaction as it occurs.

   (B) To ensure financial data is aggregated into financial statements.

   (C) To categorize transactions into specific accounts based on their nature.

   (D) To prepare financial reports for stakeholders.

3. **Which financial statement summarizes revenues and expenses to determine net income or loss?**

   (A) Balance Sheet

   (B) Income Statement

   (C) Cash Flow Statement

   (D) Statement of Owner's Equity

4. **Internal reports are primarily used for:**

    (A) Regulatory compliance.

    (B) Management decision-making and performance evaluation.

    (C) Informing external investors and creditors.

    (D) Filing tax returns.

5. **Which of the following aspects involves analyzing financial ratios and examining trends over time to derive insights?**

    (A) Recording

    (B) Classifying

    (C) Summarizing

    (D) Interpreting

Answers:

1.(C).   2.(C).   3.(B).   4.(B).   5.(D).

GOLDEN RULES OF ACCOUNTING

Financial accounting is more than just book-keeping. In accounting, every transaction has a **dual entry – debit and credit.** It is important to identify which account has to be credited and which one debited. This is the dual entry system of accounting. Financial accounting revolves around **three rules**, known as the **Golden Rules of Accounting**. These golden rules ensure systematic recording of financial transactions. The golden rules simplify the complex book-keeping rules into a set of principles that are easily understood, studied, and applied.

4.1 Types of Accounts

The golden rules of accounting help in documenting the financial transactions in ledgers. These golden rules are based on the type of account. Each transaction will have a debit and credit entry and belong to one of the following three types of accounts.

- Real Account

- Personal Account

- Nominal Account

1. Real Account

A real account is a general ledger account that reflects all the transactions relating to assets and liabilities. It comprises tangible and intangible assets. Tangible assets such as furniture, land, building, machinery, etc. On the other hand, intangible assets such as goodwill, copyright, patents, etc.

Real accounts are carried forward to the following year, therefore, are not closed at the end of the <u>financial year</u>. Furthermore, a real account appears in the <u>balance sheet</u>. A furniture account is a type of real account.

2. **Personal Account**

A personal account is a general ledger account relating to persons. It can be natural persons like individuals or artificial persons like companies, firms, associations, etc. When company ABC receives money or credit from another business or individual, company ABC becomes the receiver. And, the other business or individual who gives it becomes the giver, in the case of a personal account. A creditor account is a type of personal account.

3. **Nominal Account**

A nominal account is a general ledger account relating to all business income, expenses, profit and losses. It accounts for all transactions pertaining to one fiscal year. As a result, the balances are reset to zero and can start afresh. An interest account is a type of nominal account.

4.2   The Three Rules

GOLDEN RULES OF ACCOUNTING

Golden rules of account form the basis for bookkeeping. As per the golden rules of accounting, you must ascertain the type of account for each transaction. Each type of account has its own set of rules that needs to be applied for each transaction. Following are the three golden rules of accounting:

- o **Real Account:** Debit What Comes In, Credit What Goes Out

- o **Personal Account:** Debit the Receiver, Credit the Giver.

- o **Nominal Account:** Debit All Expenses and Losses, Credit all Incomes and Gains.

1. Debit What Comes In, Credit What Goes Out.

This rule applies to real accounts. Furniture, land, buildings, machinery, etc., are included in **real accounts.** By default, they have a debit balance. As a result, debiting what is coming in adds to the existing account balance. Similarly, when a tangible asset leaves the firm, crediting what goes out reduces the account balance.

For example, Company X sells its machinery for Rs. 50,000 on 1st June 2023. This transaction will be recorded as follows:

Date	Account	Debit	Credit
01/06/2023	By Cash Account	Rs. 50,000	—
	To Machinery Account	–	Rs. 50,000

2. Debit the Receiver, Credit the Giver.

This rule applies to **personal accounts.** When a real or artificial person pays something to the organisation, it becomes an inflow, and the person must be credited in the books. Conversely, the receiver must be debited.

For example, Company "X" paid INR 1,10,000 in Bank to "Y" Ltd. on 3nd September 2023 against supply of goods. This transaction will be recorded as follows:

Date	Account	Debit	Credit
03/09/2023	**By Y Ltd. Account**	Rs. 1,10,000	—
	To Bank Account	–	Rs. 1,10,000

3. Debit All Expenses and Losses, Credit all Incomes and Gains.

This rule applies to **nominal accounts.** A company's capital is its liability. As a result, it has a credit balance. Crediting all the income and gains will increase the capital. On the other hand, the capital reduces when expenses and losses are debited.

For example, Company X pays rent worth INR 75,000 in Bank of Z Ltd. on August 1st 2023. This transaction will be recorded as follows:

Date	Account	Debit	Credit
1/8/2023	**By Rent Account**	Rs. 75,000	—
	To Z Ltd. Account	–	Rs. 75,000

Summing Up

Golden Rules of Accounting	Real Account	Personal Account	Nominal Account
Debit	What comes in	The receiver	All expenses and losses
Credit	What goes out	The giver	All incomes and gains

Example

Let's understand the nature of the golden rules and the accounts with the help of an example. Following are the list of transactions:

- Company X starts its business with a capital of INR 1,00,000.

- Rents a property worth INR 25,000.

- Purchases goods worth INR 50,000 on credit from Company Y.

- Sells goods worth INR 75,000.

- Pays cash for goods purchased from Company Y.

- Pays salary worth INR 50,000 to employees.

Firstly, let us identify the different accounts involved and the types of accounts for each of the transactions:

Transactions	Accounts Involved	Types of Accounts
Capital of INR 1,00,000	Cash A/c; Capital A/c	Real Account; Personal Account
Rent worth INR 25,000	Rent A/c; Cash A/c	Nominal Account; Real Account
Purchases goods worth INR 50,000 on credit from Company Y	Purchases A/c; Company Y A/c	Nominal Account; Personal Account
Sells goods worth INR 75,000	Cash A/c; Sales A/c	Real Account; Nominal Account
Pays cash for goods purchased from Company Y	Company Y A/c; Cash A/c	Personal Account; Real Account
Pays salary worth INR 50,000 to employees	Salary A/c; Cash A/c	Nominal Account; Real Account

4.3   Using the Golden Rules of Accounting

Applying the golden rules of accounting will help you determine the journal entries.

A company X starts its business with a capital of INR 1,00,000

Since cash is a tangible asset, it is part of a real account. Capital is a personal account. As per the golden rule of real and personal accounts:

- Debit what comes in

- Credit the giver

Account	Dr	Cr
By Cash A/c	1,00,000	-
To Capital A/c	-	1,00,000

Rents a property worth INR 25,000

Rent is an expense and hence belongs to a nominal account. Cash is part of a real account. As per the golden rule of nominal and real accounts:

- Debit all expenses and losses

- Credit what goes out

Account	Dr	Cr
By Rent A/c	25,000	-
To Cash A/c	-	25,000

Purchases goods worth INR 50,000 on credit from Company Y

Purchase transactions are an expense, and hence they are part of a nominal account. Company Y is part of the personal account. As per the golden rule of nominal and personal accounts:

- Debit all expenses and losses

- Credit the giver

Account	Dr	Cr
By Purchases A/c	50,000	-
To Company Y A/c	-	50,000

Sells goods worth INR 75,000

Selling goods generates income for the business, and hence it is part of the nominal account. Cash is part of a real account. As per the golden rule of real and nominal accounts:

- Debit what comes in
- Credit all income and gains

Account	Dr	Cr
By Cash A/c	75,000	-
To Sales A/c	-	75,000

Pays cash for goods purchased from Company Y

Company Y is a personal account, and cash is part of a real account. As per the golden rule of personal and real accounts:

- Debit the receiver

- Credit what goes out

Account	Dr	Cr
By Company Y A/c	50,000	-
To Cash A/c	-	50,000

Pays salary worth INR 50,000 to employees

Salary is an expense to the business and hence is part of the nominal account. Cash is part of a real account. As per the golden rule of nominal and real accounts:

- Debit all expenses and losses

- Credit what goes out

Account	Dr	Cr
By Salary A/c	50,000	-
To Cash A/c	-	50,000

* * *

The above rules provide clarity on the classification of accounting, which is key to an accounts management system. Now, an SME entrepreneur will understand the **summarizing** & **interpretating** of transactions, where all recorded transactions are structured into a Balance Sheet and a Profit & Loss Statement.

* * *

Chapter Challenge: Test Your Understanding with MCQs

1. **Which type of account reflects transactions related to assets and liabilities?**

   (A) Personal Account

   (B) Nominal Account

   (C) Real Account

   (D) Artificial Account

2. **According to the golden rule, "Debit What Comes In, Credit What Goes Out," which type of account does it apply to?**

   (A) Nominal Account

   (B) Personal Account

   (C) Artificial Account

   (D) Real Account

3. **When a company receives money or credit from another business or individual, which account is credited according to the golden rule?**

   (A) Cash Account

   (B) Receivable Account

   (C) Giver's Account

   (D) Receiver's Account

4. **Which type of account relates to business income, expenses, profits, and losses?**

   (A) Personal Account

   (B) Real Account

   (C) Nominal Account

   (D) Artificial Account

5. **According to the golden rule, "Debit the Receiver, Credit the Giver," which type of account does it apply to?**

   (A) Personal Account

   (B) Real Account

   (C) Nominal Account

   (D) Artificial Account

6. **What entry is made when a company pays rent for a property it has rented?**

   (A) Debit Rent Account, Credit Cash Account

   (B) Debit Cash Account, Credit Rent Account

   (C) Debit Cash Account, Credit Bank Account

   (D) Debit Bank Account, Credit Cash Account

7. **According to the golden rule, "Debit All Expenses and Losses, Credit all Incomes and Gains," which type of account does it apply to?**

   (A) Personal Account

   (B) Real Account

   (C) Nominal Account

   (D) Artificial Account

8. **When a company sells goods On credit, which account is debited according to the golden rule?**

   (A) Sales Account

   (B) Cash Account

   (C) Gains Account

   (D) Receivable Account

9. **What entry is made when a company pays Salary in cash to its employees?**

    (A) Debit Salary Account, Credit Cash Account

    (B) Debit Cash Account, Credit Salary Account

    (C) Debit Salary Account, Credit Bank Account

    (D) Debit Bank Account, Credit Cash Account

10. **Which type of account is not closed at the end of the financial year and appears in the balance sheet?**

    (A) Nominal Account

    (B) Personal Account

    (C) Real Account

    (D) Artificial Account

Answers:

1.(C),	2.(D),	3.(C),	4.(C),	5.(A),
6.(A),	7.(C),	8.(D),	9.(A)	10.(C)

CHAPTER 05

UNDERSTANDING THE FINANCIAL STATEMENT

To understand the Financial Statement first understand the Structure:

Format of Balance Sheet (Vertical)

ABC & CO.

ADDRESS:...........

Balance Sheet as at 31st March, 2024

		(Rs. In Lacs)
Particulars	**Note No**	**As at 31st March 2024**	**As at 31 March, 2023**
I. EQUITY AND LIABILITIES			
(1) Shareholder's Funds			
(a) Share Capital	1	200.00	200.00
(b) Reserves and Surplus	2	89.50	60.00
(c) Money received against share warrants		0.00	0.00
(2) Share Application Money Pending Allotment		0.00	0.00
(3) Non-Current Liabilities			
(a) Long-term borrowings	3	180.00	200.00
(b) Deferred tax liabilities (Net)		0.00	0.00
(c) Other Long term liabilities		0.00	0.00
(d) Long term provisions		0.00	0.00
(4) Current Liabilities			
(a) Short-term borrowings	4	100.00	100.00
(b) Trade payables	5	40.00	25.00
(c) Other current liabilities	6	8.00	5.00
(d) Short-term provisions	7	11.50	8.75
TOTAL		**629.00**	**598.75**

			(Rs. In Lacs)
Particulars	**Note No**	**As at 31st March 2024**	**As at 31 March, 2023**
II.ASSETS			
(1) Non-current assets			
(a) Property, Plant & Equipment			
(i) Tangible assets	8	390.00	400.00
(ii) Intangible assets	9	3.00	3.00
(iii) Capital work-in-progress		0.00	0.00
(iv) Intangible assets under development		0.00	0.00
(b) Non-current investments	10	20.00	15.00
(c) Deferred tax assets (net)			
(d) Long term loans and advances	12	40.00	40.00
(e) Other non-current assets		0.00	0.00
(2) Current assets			
(a) Current investments		0.00	0.00
(b) Inventories	13	86.00	41.00
(c) Trade receivables	14	80.00	70.00
(d) Cash and cash equivalents	15	5.00	15.75
(e) Short-term loans and advances	16	3.50	14.00
(f) Other current assets	17	1.50	0.00
TOTAL		**629.00**	**598.75**

Format of Balance Sheet (Horizontal)
ABC & CO.
ADDRESS.................

BALANCE SHEET
AS AT 31ST MARCH 2024

					(Rs. In Lacs)
Equity & Liabilities	Amount	Amount	Assets	Amount	Amount
Proprietor's Fund:			**Property, Plant & Equipment:** (Including Intangible Assets of Rs. 3.00 Lacs)		393.00
Capital A/c	260.00		**Non-Current Assets**		
Add: Net profit for the year	34.50				
	294.50		FDR	20.00	60.00
Less: Drawings	5.00	289.50	Loans & Advances	40.00	
Secured Loans			**Current Assets**		
Term Loan from Bank		180.00	Stock-in-hand	86.00	
CC Limit from Bank		100.00	Cash In Bank	4.00	
			Cash in Hand	1.00	
Current Liabilities & Provisions:			Sundry Debtors	80.00	
			Advance to Suppliers	3.50	
Sundry Creditors		40.00	GST Receivable	1.50	176.00
Advance from Customers		6.00			
Other Provisions		2.00			
Income Tax Payable		11.50			
TOTAL		629.00	**TOTAL**		629.00

Note:

1. Vertical format is generally used by the Corporate Entities and horizontal format presented over here are generally used by the proprietorship firm

2. To understand it better, figures of Both the formats are kept same

3. The above format and figures are for academic purpose only

4. There are some further breakups required as per the statutory provisions on the face of Balance Sheet like Sundry Creditors needs to be bifurcated for MSME & Others but for the sake of convenience the same is not presented here

5. Note No. mentioned in Vertical Format is indicative only and require detail schedules as prescribed under the Companies Act.

6. Readers of the Balance Sheet may look into the provisions & schedules as per Companies Act, Guidance notes of ICAI & other explanatory statement for advance level understanding & presentation of Balance Sheet

Reading a balance sheet is crucial for understanding the financial health of a business. For an SME entrepreneur in India, breaking down the balance sheet into simpler, manageable parts can make the task easier. Here's a step-by-step guide to reading a balance sheet item-wise. For the sake of convenience value is written against each line items from the Draft format of Balance Sheet mentioned above:

5.1   Understanding the Balance Sheet Structure

A balance sheet is divided into three main sections:

- o   **Equity**: The owner's stake in the company.

- o   **Liabilities:** What the company owes.

- o   **Total Assets**: What the company owns.

Examine Equity (Rs. 289.50 Lacs):

Equity represents the owner's stake in the company.

- **Share Capital**: The money invested by the owners or shareholders.

- **Retained Earnings**: Profits that have been reinvested in the business rather than distributed as dividends or withdrawal by proprietor.

- **Reserves and Surplus**: Portions of profit set aside for specific purposes or general reserves.

Examine the Liabilities (Rs. 339.50 Lacs):

Liabilities are also divided into **Current Liabilities** and **Non-Current Liabilities**.

a. **Current Liabilities (Rs. 159.50 lacs):**

    o **Accounts Payable**: Money the business owes to suppliers.

    o **Short-term Debt**: Loans and borrowings due within a year like CC Limit from Bank

    o **Accrued Liabilities**: Expenses that have been incurred but not yet paid. For Eg. Sundry Creditors & Other Provisions

b. **Non-Current Liabilities (Rs. 180.00 Lacs):**

    o **Long-term Debt**: Loans and borrowings that are due after one year. For Eg. Term Loan from Bank for Purchase of Machinery

Examine the Assets (Rs. 629.00 Lacs)

Assets are typically divided into **Current Assets** and **Non-Current Assets**.

a. **Current Assets (Rs. 176.00 Lacs):**

    o **Cash and Cash Equivalents**: The most liquid assets, including cash in hand and bank balances.

    o **Trade Receivable/ Sundry Debtors**: Money owed to the business by customers.

    o **Inventory**: Goods available for sale.

    o **Other Current Assets**: Payments made in advance for goods or services to be received in the future. For Eg: Advance to Supplier and GST Receivable

b. **Non-Current Assets (Rs. 453.00 Lacs):**

    o **Property, Plant, and Equipment (PP&E)**: Long-term investments in physical assets like machinery, buildings, etc.

- o **Intangible Assets**: Non-physical assets such as patents, trademarks, and goodwill.

- o **Long-term Investments**: Investments that the company intends to hold for over a year. For Eg: FDR, Long term Loans & Advances like Advance for Purchase of Property etc

Format of Profit & Loss Statement (Vertical)

1. ABC & CO.
ADDRESS:………..
Profit and Loss statement for the year ended 31st March, 2024

			(Rs. In Lacs)
Particulars	Note No	Figures as at the end of 31st March 2024	Figures as at the end of 31st March 2023
I. Revenue from operations (Gross)	18	325.00	220.00
Less: Excise Duty		-	-
Revenue from operations (Net)		325.00	220.00
II. Other Income	19	0.00	0.00
III. Total Revenue (I +II)		**325.00**	**220.00**
IV. Expenses:			
Cost of materials consumed	20	0.00	0.00
Purchase of Stock-in-Trade	21	194.00	100.00
Changes in inventories of finished goods, work-in-progress and Stock-in-Trade	22	(45.00)	(30.00)
Employee benefit expense	23	45.00	40.00
Financial costs	24	30.00	25.00
Depreciation and amortization expense	25	10.00	12.00
Preliminary and Preoperative Exp.		0.00	0.00
Other expenses (Incl. Direct Exp. Of Rs. 10.00 Lacs)	26	45.00	38.00
Total Expenses		**279.00**	**185.00**

Particulars	Note No	Figures as at the end of 31st March 2024	Figures as at the end of 31st March 2023 (Rs. In Lacs)
V. Profit before exceptional and extraordinary items and tax	(III - IV)	46.00	35.00
VI. Exceptional Items		0.00	0.00
VII. Profit before extraordinary items and tax (V + VI)		46.00	35.00
VIII. Extraordinary Items		0.00	0.00
IX. Profit before tax (VII + VIII)		**46.00**	**35.00**
X. Tax expense:			
(1) Current tax	27	11.50	8.75
(2) Deferred tax Liabilities / (Assets)		0.00	0.00
XI. Profit(Loss) from the period from continuing operations	(IX + X))	34.50	26.25
XII. Profit/(Loss) from discontinuing operations		0.00	0.00
XIII. Tax expense of discounting operations		0.00	0.00
XIV. Profit/(Loss) from Discontinuing operations (XII - XIII)		0.00	0.00
XV. Profit/(Loss) for the period (XI + XIV)		**34.50**	**26.25**
XVI. Earning per equity share:			
(1) Basic		1.73	1.31
(2) Diluted		1.73	1.31

Format of Profit & Loss Statement (Horizontal)

ABC & CO.

ADDRESS................

TRADING, PROFIT AND LOSS ACCOUNT

FOR THE PERIOD ENDED 31/03/2024

			(Rs. In Lacs)
Particulars	**Amount**	**Particulars**	**Amount**
To Opening Stock	41.00	**By Sales**	325.00
To Purchases	194.00	By Closing Stock	86.00
To Direct Expenses	10.00		
To Gross Profit C/D	166.00		
	411.00		**411.00**
To Salary & wages	45.00	By Gross Profit B/D	166.00
To Telephone & Mobile Charges	0.50		
To Printing & Stationary	2.00		
To Insurance Charge	3.00		
To Repair & Maintenance Exp	0.80		
To Shop Exp	13.85		
To Power & Fuel Charges	12.50		
To Bank Interest & Charges	30.00		
To Depreciation	10.00		
To Legal Charge	2.00		
To Audit Fee	0.25		
To Miscellaneous Exp.	0.10		
To Net Profit C/D	46.00		
	166.00		**166.00**
To Provision for Tax	11.50	By Net Profit B/D	46.00
To Net Profit Transferred to proprietors Capital A/c	34.50		
	46.00		**46.00**

The indirect expenses rows (from "To Salary & wages" through "To Miscellaneous Exp.") are bracketed and labelled **INDIRECT EXPENSES**.

Note:

2. Vertical format is generally used by the Corporate Entities and horizontal format presented over here are generally used by the proprietorship firm

3. To understand it better figures of Both the formats are kept same

4. The above format and figures are for academic purpose only

5. Note No. mentioned in Vertical Format is indicative only and require detail schedules as prescribed under the Companies Act.

6. Readers of the Profit & Loss Statement may look into the provisions & schedules as per Companies Act, Guidance notes of ICAI & other explanatory statement for advance level understanding & presentation of Profit & Loss Statement

5.2   Understanding the Profit & Loss Statement Structure

A Profit & Loss statement is having Top Line & Bottom Line as below. Figures against each item is mentioned from the Draft Format of Profit & Loss Account mentioned above:

Revenue- The Topline (Rs. 325.00 Lacs)

-   **Revenue (or Sales):** The total amount of money generated from selling goods or services before any expenses are deducted. It's often referred to as the "top line" because it appears at the top of the income statement.

Cost of Goods Sold (COGS) (Rs. 159.00 Lacs)

-   **Cost of Goods Sold (COGS):** The direct costs attributable to the production of the goods sold by a company. This includes the cost of materials consumed (after adjustment of Stock held by the entity) and labour or other direct expenses directly used to create the product. It does not include indirect expenses such as distribution costs and sales force costs.

Gross Profit (Rs. 166.00 Lacs)

- **Gross Profit**: The difference between revenue and COGS. It represents the profit a company makes after deducting the costs associated with making and selling its products or the costs associated with providing its services.

  o **Formula**: Gross Profit = Revenue - COGS

Indirect Expenses (Rs. 120.00 Lacs)

- **Indirect Expenses**: The costs required to run a company that are not directly tied to the production of goods or services. This includes salaries, rent, utilities, and other day-to-day expenses.

EBITDA (Rs. 86.00 Lacs)

- **EBITDA (Earnings Before Interest, Taxes, Depreciation, and Amortization)**: A measure of a company's overall financial performance and is used as an alternative to net income in some circumstances. It strips out the cost of debt capital and its tax effects by adding back interest and taxes to earnings, as well as adding back depreciation and amortization.

  o **Formula**: EBITDA = Net Profit before Tax + Interest + Depreciation + Amortization

Net Profit After Tax- The Bottom Line (Rs. 34.50 Lacs)

- **Net Profit (or Net Income)**: The actual profit after working expenses not included in the calculation of gross profit have been paid. It is often referred to as the "bottom line" because it is found at the bottom of the income statement. Net profit includes all revenues and gains, expenses and losses, and taxes.

  o **Formula**: Net Profit = Total Revenue - Total Expenses- Taxes

Additional Terms

1. **Depreciation and Amortization (Rs. 10.00 Lacs):**

    o   **Depreciation**: The reduction in the value of a tangible asset over time due to use and wear and tear.

    o   **Amortization**: The reduction in the value of an intangible asset over time or the process of spreading the cost of an intangible asset over its useful life.

2. **Interest Expense (Rs. 30.00 Lacs)**: The cost incurred by an entity for borrowed funds. It is essentially the interest payable on any borrowings – bonds, loans, convertible debt, or lines of credit.

3. **Tax Expense (Rs. 11.50 Lacs)**: The total amount of tax that a company is liable to pay to the government in a given period. This can include both current tax and deferred tax.

4. **Earnings Per Share (EPS) (1.73)**: A company's profit divided by the outstanding shares of its common stock. EPS serves as an indicator of a company's profitability.

    o   **Formula**: EPS = Net Profit / Number of Outstanding Shares

* * *

Chapter Challenge: Test Your Understanding with MCQs

1. **What does Share Capital represent in a balance sheet?**

   (A) Money owed to the business by customers

   (B) Money invested by the owners or shareholders

   (C) Long-term borrowings

   (D) Current investments

2. **Which section of the balance sheet includes Accounts Payable?**

   (A) Shareholder's Funds

   (B) Non-Current Liabilities

   (C) Current Liabilities

   (D) Non-Current Assets

3. **What are Non-Current Assets typically composed of?**

   (A) Short-term borrowings

   (B) Cash and cash equivalents

   (C) Long-term investments

   (D) Trade receivables

4. **What does "Gross Profit" represent in a Profit & Loss statement?**

   (A) The total amount of money generated from selling goods or services

   (B) The difference between revenue and Cost of Goods Sold (COGS)

   (C) The costs required to run a company that are not directly tied to production

   (D) The actual profit after working expenses not included in the calculation of gross profit have been paid

5. **Which term represents the reduction in the value of a tangible asset over time due to use and wear and tear?**

(A) Amortization

(B) Depreciation

(C) Gross Profit

(D) EBITDA

6. **What does EBITDA stand for?**

(A) Earnings Before Interest, Taxes, Dividends, and Amortization

(B) Earnings Before Interest, Taxes, Depreciation, and Amortization

(C) Extraordinary Items Before Interest, Taxes, Dividends, and Amortization

(D) Earnings Before Income, Taxes, Depreciation, and Assets

7. **Which expense represents the cost incurred by an entity for borrowed funds?**

(A) Indirect Expenses

(B) Depreciation

(C) Tax Expense

(D) Interest Expense

8. **What does Net Profit represent in a Profit & Loss statement?**

(A) The total revenue of the company

(B) The difference between revenue and COGS

(C) The actual profit after all expenses and taxes have been paid

(D) The cost of goods sold

9. What is the formula for calculating Earnings Per Share (EPS)?

(A) EPS = Gross Profit / Total Revenue

(B) EPS = Net Profit / Number of Outstanding Shares

(C) EPS = Total Expenses / Total Revenue

(D) EPS = Net Profit / Gross Profit

10. Which section of the balance sheet includes the term "Share Application Money Pending Allotment"?

(A) Non-Current Liabilities

(B) Shareholder's Funds

(C) Current Liabilities

(D) Non-Current Assets

Answers

1.(B),   2.(C),   3.(C),   4.(B),   5.(B),
6.(B),   7.(D),   8.(C),   9.(B)   10.(B)

INTERPRETING THE ACCOUNTS-FINANCIAL ANALYSIS

Financial analysis is a critical skill for understanding the financial health and performance of a business. It involves examining financial statements—balance sheets, income statements, and cash flow statements—to assess a company's profitability, liquidity, leverage, and activity efficiency. This analysis provides valuable insights for stakeholders, including investors, creditors, and management, facilitating informed decision-making.

Broadly these Financial Ratios/ Accounting Ratios are as below:

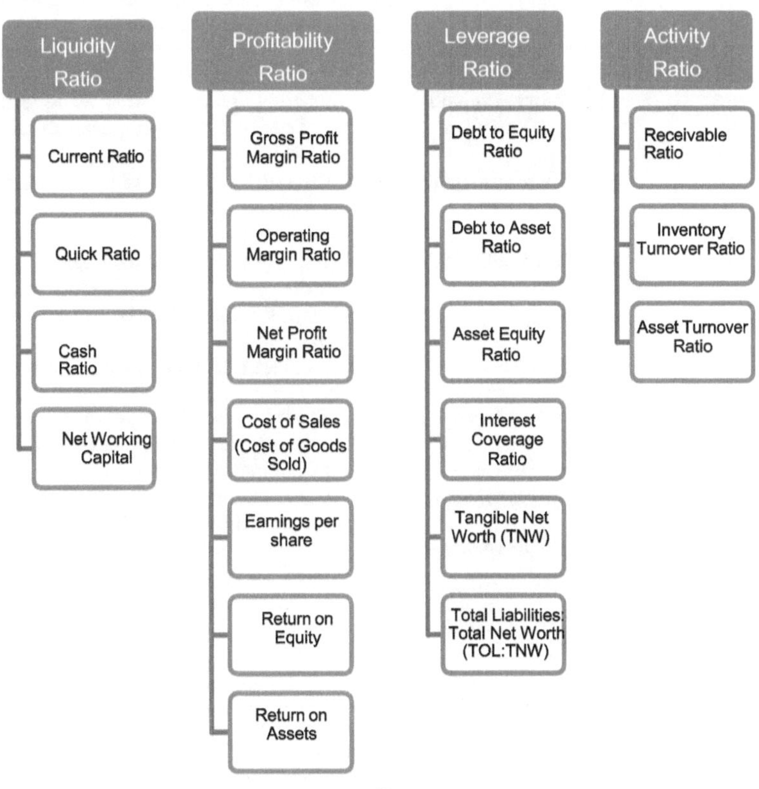

	Let's Evaluate one by one formula by taking example of Financial Statement of previous Chapter		
	Particulars	**Formula**	**Description**
A.	**Liquidity Ratio**		• Liquidity ratio helps in measuring the cash sufficiency of an enterprise to pay off its short-term liabilities. • A High liquidity ratio ensures the company is in a good position to pay its creditors. • The liquid ratio of 2 or more is considered acceptable.
1.	Current Ratio (CR) Or Working Capital Ratio.	$$= \frac{\text{Current Assets}}{\text{Current Liabilities}}$$ **Ans:** (176.00/159.50) **= 1.10**	• This is a liquidity ratio that measures a company's ability to pay short-term obligations or those due within one year. • A current ratio that is in line with the industry average or higher is generally considered acceptable. • In the present case the same is 1.10 as Current Assets are slightly higher than the current liabilities. Considering the Banks Working Capital Finance is available at 10% approx. this ratio is adequate otherwise if higher margin in required then promoters need to infuse fresh capital as margin to bring in line with the Banks Benchmark
2.	Quick Ratio (QR) Or Acid Test Ratio	$$= \frac{\text{Current Assets- Inventory- Prepaid Expenses}}{\text{Current Liabilities}}$$ **Ans:** (90.00/159.50)= **0.56**	• It indicates the company's ability to instantly use its near-cash assets (assets that can be converted quickly to cash) to pay down its current liabilities. • The quick ratio is considered a more conservative measure than the current ratio, which includes all current assets as coverage for current liabilities • in the present Case it is Less than 1, hence it is likely that the company's financial health is weak and it can't pay off its current liabilities comfortably.
3.	Cash Ratio	$$= \frac{\text{Cash + Marketable Securities}}{\text{Current Liabilities}}$$ **Ans:** (5.00/159.50)= **0.03**	• This ratio considers only those current assets which are immediately available to the company to pay its debts. • A ratio above 1 indicates that a company can pay off its current liabilities with cash and have funds left over, while a ratio of 0.5 to 1 is usually preferred. A higher cash ratio can indicate less credit and liquidity risk, but a ratio that's too high could also indicate mismanagement or misallocated capital

	Let's Evaluate one by one formula by taking example of Financial Statement of previous Chapter		
	Particulars	**Formula**	**Description**
4.	Net Working Capital (NWC)	= Current Assets- Current Liabilities **Ans:** (176.00- 159.50)= **16.50**	• It gives an idea of a business's liquidity and whether the company has enough money to cover its short-term obligations. • If the net working capital figure is zero or greater, the business is able to cover its current obligations.
B.	**Profitability Ratio**		• Profitability ratiis generally used to determine how well the business is generating profits from its operations.
1.	Gross Profit Margin	$$= \frac{\text{Gross Profit*}}{\text{Revenue}}$$ *Gross profit= Revenue - COGS **Ans:** (166.00/325.00* 100)= **51.07%**	• It is a metric analysts use to assess a company's financial health by calculating the amount of money left over from product sales after subtracting the cost of goods sold (COGS).
2.	Operating Margin	$$= \frac{\text{Gross Profit - Operating Expenses}}{\text{Revenue}}$$ **Ans:** (76.00/325.00*100)= **23.38%**	• Unlike Gross profit ratio, this includes more expenses and hence it is used to ascertain company's profitability more efficiently. • From the gross profits, operating expenses such as selling and distribution cost, administration cost etc. are deducted to arrive at operating margin
3.	Net Profit Margin	$$= \frac{\text{Net Profit}}{\text{Revenue}}$$ **Ans:** (46.00/325.00*100)= **14.15%**	• It is the amount of profit made after deducting selling, general, and administrative costs, from gross profit. This illustrates how much of revenue collected by a company translates into profit.
4.	Cost of Sales Or Cost of Goods Sold	= Beginning Inventory + Purchases + Direct Expenses (–) Ending Inventory **Ans:** (41.00+194.00+10.00- 86.00) = **159.00**	• It is the accumulated total of all costs used to create a product or service, which has been sold. • The cost of sales is a key part of the performance metrics of a company, since it measures the ability of an entity to design, source, and manufacture goods at a reasonable cost • It does not include any general and administrative expenses. It also does not include any costs of the sales and marketing department.

	Particulars	Formula	Description
		Let's Evaluate one by one formula by taking example of Financial Statement of previous Chapter	
5.	Earnings Per Share (EPS)	$$= \frac{\text{Net Income}}{\text{Outstanding Shares*}}$$ **Ans:** (34.50/20*)= **1.73** *Considering Rs. 10 Per Share	• EPS is more important to shareholders since it helps in determining the return on investment. • Generally weighted average Outstanding shares are used since outstanding shares can change over time • Higher the EPS, higher is the stock price of the company. • Sometime Diluted EPS are used which includes options, convertible securities and warrants outstanding which affects outstanding shares.
6.	Return on Equity (ROE)	$$= \frac{\text{Net Profit}}{(\text{Opening Equity} + \text{Closing Equity})/2}$$ **Ans:** [34.50/(289.50+ 260.00)/2]*100= 8.22%	• This is a measure of financial performance calculated by dividing net income by shareholders' equity. • It is considered a measure of the profitability of a corporation in relation to stockholders' equity.
7.	Return on Assets (ROA)	$$= \frac{\text{Net Profit}}{(\text{Opening Total Assets} + \text{Closing Total Assets})/2}$$ **Ans:** [34.50/ (629.00+598.75)/2 * 100]= **5.62%**	• This is an indicator of how profitable a company is relative to its total assets. • ROA gives a manager, investor, or analyst an idea as to how efficient a company's management is at using its assets to generate earnings. • It takes into account a company's debt, unlike other similar metrics like Return on Equity (ROE). • The higher the ROA the better.
C.	**Leverage Ratio**		• Leverage ratio measures the utilization of borrowed money by the business. It helps to identify the financial stability of the business by analyzing the total debt of the company.
1.	Debt-Equity Ratio (DER)	= Debt / Equity or = Long Term Borrowings / Capital **Ans:** (180.00/ 289.50) = **0.62: 1**	• Debt-equity ratio is the measure of the relative contribution of the creditors and shareholders or owners in the capital employed in business. • This financial tool gives an idea of how much borrowed capital (debt) can be fulfilled in the event of liquidation using shareholder contributions. • A low debt-equity ratio is favorable from investment viewpoint as it is less risky in times of increasing interest rates.

	Let's Evaluate one by one formula by taking example of Financial Statement of previous Chapter		
	Particulars	**Formula**	**Description**
2.	Debt to Asset Ratio	= Total Debt / Total Assets **Ans:** (280.00/ 629.00)= **0.44: 1**	• This can be used to determine if the business will be able to pay all of its debts if the business is closed immediately. • A company having a debt to asset ratio of less than 1 is considered as good for investment. • If the ratio is greater than 1, the company is considered as highly leveraged.
3.	Asset to Equity Ratio	$$= \frac{\text{Total Assets}}{\text{Total Equity}}$$ **Ans:** (629.00/ 289.50)= **2.17: 1**	• The asset/equity ratio indicates the relationship of the total assets of the firm to the part owned by shareholders (aka, owner's equity). This ratio is an indicator of the company's leverage (debt) used to finance the firm.
4.	Interest Coverage Ratio	$$= \frac{\text{Earning Before Interest \& Taxes (EBIT)}}{\text{Interest Expenses}}$$ **Ans:** (86.00/30.00)= **2.86**	• This ratio is used to measure the company's ability to meet its interest payment obligation • A higher ratio indicates a better financial position of the business.
5.	Tangible Net Worth (TNW)	= Equity Shareholder's Funds (-) Intangible Assets Or = Total Assets (-) Total Liabilities (-) Intangible Assets **Ans:** (289.50 - 3.00)= **286.50**	• Tangible net worth is the sum total of one's tangible assets (those that can be physically held or converted to cash) minus one's total debts. • Calculating your tangible net worth involves totaling all your assets- cash, investments, and property and totaling all your secured and unsecured debt, and then subtracting the latter from the former.
6.	Total Liabilities/ Tangible Net Worth (TOL/TNW)	= Total Liabilities/ Total Net Worth **Ans:** (339.50/ 289.50) = **1.17: 1**	• It is a measure of a company's financial leverage calculated by dividing the total liabilities of the company by the total net worth of the business. • Total outside liability is the sum of all the liabilities of the business and total net worth is the sum of share capital and surplus reserves of the company. • This ratio gives an accurate picture of the businesses reliance on debt. • A low TOL/TNW ratio signifies good levels of promoter's stake in the business, whereas a high TOL/TNW ratio shows low levels of promoter's stake in the business, which is considered risky.

<table>
<tr><td colspan="4" align="center">Let's Evaluate one by one formula by taking example of
Financial Statement of previous Chapter</td></tr>
<tr><td></td><td>Particulars</td><td>Formula</td><td>Description</td></tr>
<tr>
<td>D.</td>
<td>Activity Ratio</td>
<td></td>
<td><ul><li>Activity ratio indicates the return generated from a particular type of asset using the sales, cost and asset data.</li><li>This is also referred to as <u>Efficiency Ratio</u>.</li><li>This ratio helps the business to identify effective utilization of the assets and thereby facilitates efficient management.</li></ul></td>
</tr>
<tr>
<td>1.</td>
<td>Receivable Ratio</td>
<td>$$=\frac{\text{Average Debtors}*365}{\text{Annual Sales (Credit)}}$$ = [(80.00 + 70.00)/2 * 365/ 300.00)= 25 Days</td>
<td><ul><li>This measures how soon the firms collect its receivables.</li><li>For the ratio calculation, monthly average receivables and sales on credit terms are used generally.</li><li>A Low receivable ratio indicates the business sales collection process is working well.</li><li>Average collection period is determined using this ratio.</li></ul></td>
</tr>
<tr>
<td>2.</td>
<td>Inventory Turnover Ratio</td>
<td>$$=\frac{\text{Turnover}}{(\text{Opening stock}+\text{Closing stock})/2}$$ Ans: [325.00/ (41.00+86.00)/2] = 5.11</td>
<td><ul><li>It is a financial ratio showing how many times a company has sold and replaced inventory during a given period.</li><li>A slow turnover implies weak sales and possibly excess inventory, while a faster ratio implies either strong sales or insufficient inventory</li></ul></td>
</tr>
<tr>
<td>3.</td>
<td>Total Assets Turnover Ratio</td>
<td>$$=\frac{\text{Revenue}}{(\text{Opening Total Assets}+\text{Closing Total Assets})/2}$$ Ans: [325.00/ (629.00+598.75)/2]= 0.53</td>
<td><ul><li>This can be used as an indicator of the efficiency with which a company is using its assets to generate revenue.</li><li>The higher the asset turnover ratio, the more efficient a company is at generating revenue from its assets. Conversely, if a company has a low asset turnover ratio, it indicates it is not efficiently using its assets to generate sales.</li><li>A company's asset turnover ratio can be impacted by large asset sales as well as significant asset purchases in a given year.</li></ul></td>
</tr>
</table>

Readers of the above Financial Ratios are advised to practice more and more each component of the financial statement and check the trend and ratio with the corresponding previous year. This helps in making Better understanding of Interpreting the Accounts and helpful in decision making.

* * *

Chapter Challenge: Test Your Understanding with MCQs

1. **What does the Current Ratio measure?**

   (A) Long-term liquidity

   (B) Short-term liquidity

   (C) Profitability

   (D) Efficiency

2. **Which ratio is considered a more conservative measure of liquidity than the Current Ratio?**

   (A) Quick Ratio

   (B) Cash Ratio

   (C) Net Working Capital

   (D) Debt-Equity Ratio

3. **What does the Gross Profit Margin indicate?**

   (A) The efficiency of asset utilization

   (B) The company's ability to cover long-term debts

   (C) The percentage of revenue remaining after deducting the cost of goods sold

   (D) The company's ability to pay off current liabilities instantly

4. **What does the Debt-Equity Ratio measure?**

   (A) Efficiency of asset utilization

   (B) Short-term liquidity

   (C) Relative contribution of creditors and shareholders to the capital employed

   (D) Profitability

5. Which ratio measures how efficiently a company is using its assets to generate revenue?

(A) Current Ratio

(B) Total Assets Turnover Ratio

(C) Debt-Equity Ratio

(D) Return on Equity

6. What does the Receivable Ratio measure?

(A) Average collection period

(B) Inventory turnover

(C) Efficiency of asset utilization

(D) Liquidity

7. What does the Return on Equity (ROE) measure?

(A) Efficiency of asset utilization

(B) Short-term liquidity

(C) Profitability in relation to shareholders' equity

(D) Ability to meet interest payment obligations

8. Which ratio indicates the return generated from a particular type of asset using the sales, cost, and asset data?

(A) Debt-Equity Ratio

(B) Receivable Ratio

(C) Inventory Turnover Ratio

(D) Total Assets Turnover Ratio

9. What does the Tangible Net Worth represent?

    (A) Total assets minus total liabilities

    (B) Total assets minus intangible assets

    (C) Total liabilities minus total assets

    (D) Total equity minus intangible assets

10. What does the Interest Coverage Ratio measure?

    (A) The ability to meet short-term obligations

    (B) The ability to meet interest payment obligations

    (C) The efficiency of asset utilization

    (D) The liquidity position of the company

Answers

1.(B),	2.(A),	3.(C),	4.(C),	5.(B),
6.(A),	7.(C),	8.(B),	9.(B),	10.(B)

DEEP DIVE TO THE WORLD OF ACCOUNTING: SOME IMPORTANT CONCEPTS

After understanding the basics of the profit and loss statement and the balance sheet with Financial Ratios, it's crucial to delve deeper into specific accounting concepts. These concepts ensure accurate accounting methods and prevent classification errors, essential for SME entrepreneurs.

7.1   Cash vs. Accrual Accounting: Cash accounting records revenues and expenses when they are actually received or paid. Accrual accounting, on the other hand, records revenues and expenses when they are earned or incurred, regardless of when the cash transaction happens. Accrual accounting provides a more accurate financial picture of the company's performance.

7.2 Revenue Expenditure vs. Capital Expenditure: Revenue expenditures are short-term expenses incurred during the regular operations of the business, which are fully expensed in the accounting period. Capital expenditures, however, are long-term investments in assets that will benefit the business for multiple periods. Properly distinguishing between these ensures the correct allocation of expenses over time.

7.3 Expenses vs. Loans and Advances (Assets): Expenses are costs incurred in the ordinary course of business to generate revenue and are recorded on the income statement. Loans and advances, however, are amounts provided by the business to others, expecting future repayment, and are recorded as assets on the balance sheet. Proper classification ensures clarity in financial reporting.

7.4 Income vs. Loans and Advances (Liabilities): Income is the money earned by the business from its core operations, recorded on the income statement. Loans and advances (liabilities), in contrast, are funds borrowed by the business, which must be repaid in the future, and are recorded on the balance sheet. Understanding this distinction helps in accurately reflecting the company's financial obligations and revenue.

This chapter aims to equip SME entrepreneurs with a thorough understanding of essential accounting concepts such as Cash vs. Accrual Accounting, Expenses vs. Loans and Advances (Assets), Income vs. Loans and Advances (Liabilities), and Revenue Expenditure vs. Capital Expenditure. Grasping these concepts will aid in accurate accounting practices and help avoid common errors in financial classification. Now Let us discuss each Item in Detail & remember Golden Rules of Accounting Discussed previously.

7.1 Cash Vs. Accrual

Cash Method of Accounting

Definition: In the cash method of accounting, revenues and expenses are recorded only when cash is actually received or paid. This method is straightforward and is often used by small businesses and individuals.

How It Works:

- **Revenue Recognition**: Revenue is recorded when cash is received, not when the sale is made.

- **Expense Recognition**: Expenses are recorded when cash is paid, not when the obligation is incurred.

Example: Imagine you run a small grocery store in Mumbai. Here's how you would record transactions using the cash method:

- **Revenue Example**: You sell goods worth ₹10,000 to a customer on credit in 20th April 2024. The customer pays you in 03rd May 2024. Under the cash method, you record the ₹10,000 revenue in May, when you actually receive the cash. No voucher to be passed on 20th April 2024.

Voucher to be entered in the books of accounts on 03rd May 2024:

Particular	Debit	Credit
By Cash A/c	10000.00	
To Sales A/c		10000.00

- **Expense Example:** You purchase inventory worth ₹5,000 on credit in 05th March 2024 and pay the bill in 11th April 2024. Under the cash method, you record the ₹5,000 expense in April, when you pay the cash, not in March when you receive the inventory.

Voucher to be entered in the books of accounts on 11th April 2024:

Particular	Debit	Credit
By Purchase A/c	5000.00	
To Cash A/c		5000.00

Industries Preferring Cash Method:

- **Very Small Retail Stores**: Grocery stores, convenience shops, and other small-scale retail operations.

- **Personal Service Providers**: Freelancers, consultants, hairdressers, and other professionals who provide personal services and have straightforward transactions.

- **Small Restaurants and Cafes**: Businesses with direct and immediate cash transactions from customers.

- **Local Repair Shops**: Car repair shops, electronic repair shops, and other small repair services.

All other small traders & service providers who do not maintain regular Books of Accounts &/or exempt from GST & other Indirect Taxes compliances.

Accrual Method of Accounting

Definition: In the accrual method of accounting, revenues and expenses are recorded when they are earned or incurred, regardless of when the cash transaction happens. This method provides a more accurate picture of a company's financial position and performance.

How It Works:

- **Revenue Recognition**: Revenue is recorded when earned, even if the cash hasn't been received yet.

- **Expense Recognition**: Expenses are recorded when incurred, even if the cash hasn't been paid yet.

Example: Using the same grocery store example in Mumbai, here's how transactions would be recorded using the accrual method:

- **Revenue Example**: You sell goods worth ₹10,000 to a customer on credit in 20th April 2024. The customer pays you in 03rd May 2024. Even though the customer pays you in May, you record the ₹10,000 revenue in April, when the sale is made and the revenue is earned.

Voucher to be entered in the books of accounts on 20th April 2024:

Particular	Debit	Credit
By Customer A/c	10000.00	
To Sales A/c		10000.00

Voucher to be entered in the books of accounts on 03rd May 2024:

Particular	Debit	Credit
By Cash A/c	10000.00	
To Customer A/c		10000.00

- **Expense Example**: You purchase inventory worth ₹5,000 on credit on 05th March 2024 and pay the bill in 11th April 2024. Under the accrual method, you record the ₹5,000 expense in March, when you receive the inventory and incur the obligation, not in April when you pay the cash.

Voucher to be entered in the books of accounts on 05th March 2024:

Particular	Debit	Credit
By Purchase A/c	5000.00	
To Supplier A/c		5000.00

Voucher to be entered in the books of accounts on 11th April 2024:

Particular	Debit	Credit
By Supplier A/c	5000.00	
To Cash A/c		5000.00

Industries Preferring Accrual Method:

- **Manufacturing**: Companies that deal with production and inventory, requiring detailed tracking of costs and revenues.

- **IT and Software**: Businesses that provide services on a project basis, often dealing with large contracts and long-term projects.

- **Telecommunications**: Companies with extensive infrastructure and long-term service contracts.

- **Real Estate**: Firms dealing with property development, sales, and rentals, where transactions often span over long periods.

- **Finance and Insurance**: Institutions that need to match revenues with the periods they are earned to provide accurate financial reporting.

- **Medium to Large size business**: Retailers with complex operations, inventory management, and credit sales.

All other who does maintain regular Books of Accounts & in compliance to the various statutory provisions & Taxes such as GST Etc.

Comparison

Aspect	Cash Method of Accounting	Accrual Method of Accounting
Revenue Recognition	When cash is received	When revenue is earned, regardless of when cash is received
Expense Recognition	When cash is paid	When expense is incurred, regardless of when cash is paid

Aspect	Cash Method of Accounting	Accrual Method of Accounting
Complexity	Simple and straightforward	More complex and requires detailed tracking
Cash Flow Tracking	Directly tracks cash flow	Does not directly track cash flow
Financial Position	May not reflect true financial position	Provides a more accurate picture of financial position
Users	Small businesses, freelancers, consultants, personal finances	Medium to large businesses, listed companies, organizations with statutory requirements
Industries Preferring	Very Small retail stores, personal service providers, small restaurants, local repair shops	Manufacturing, IT and software, telecommunications, real estate, finance, Medium to large Stores
Regulatory Requirements	Suitable for very small businesses not mandated to follow detailed regulations	Required for companies registered under the Companies Act, 2013, and those following Ind AS
Financial Statements	May not show outstanding receivables and payables	Shows a comprehensive view including receivables and payables
Example (Revenue)	Sell goods in April, receive payment in May, record revenue in May	Sell goods in April, invoice in April, record revenue in April
Example (Expense)	Purchase inventory in March, pay in April, record expense in April	Purchase inventory in March, incur expense in March, record expense in March

7.2   Revenue Expenditure Vs. Capital Expenditure

Revenue Expenditure

Definition: Revenue expenditure refers to the costs incurred during the normal course of business operations that are intended to maintain or generate income within the current accounting period. These expenditures are typically short-term and are fully deducted from the business's income in the period they are incurred.

Characteristics:

- Short-term benefit (usually within one accounting period)

- Recurrent and regular expenses

- Related to the day-to-day operations of the business

- Recorded on the income statement as expenses

Examples:

1. **Salaries and Wages:** Payments to employees for their services during the accounting period.

   - Example: INR 50,000 paid to employees for their work in the current month.

2. **Rent and Utilities:** Costs for leasing office space and utilities consumed.

   - Example: INR 20,000 paid for office rent and electricity bills for the month.

3. **Maintenance and Repairs:** Expenses for keeping machinery and equipment in working condition.

   - Example: INR 10,000 spent on repairing machinery in the factory.

4. **Raw Materials and Inventory:** Costs of purchasing materials used in the production process.

   - Example: INR 30,000 spent on purchasing raw materials like wood, nails, and varnish for furniture production.

Illustration of Revenue Expenditure:

An SME that manufactures furniture spends INR 30,000 on raw materials like wood, nails, and varnish. These materials are used to produce furniture that will be sold within the same accounting period. This INR 30,000 is a revenue expenditure as it is necessary for generating income in the short term.

Capital Expenditure

Definition: Capital expenditure refers to funds used by a business to acquire, upgrade, or maintain long-term assets such as property, machinery, or equipment. These expenditures are expected to provide benefits over multiple accounting periods.

Characteristics:

- Long-term benefit (more than one accounting period)

- Involves large sums of money

- Adds value to the business by acquiring or enhancing assets

- Recorded on the balance sheet as assets, which are then depreciated over their useful life

Examples:

1. **Purchase of Machinery:** Buying new machinery for the production process.

   o Example: INR 5,00,000 spent on purchasing a new piece of machinery for the factory.

2. **Building Acquisition:** Purchasing or constructing new office buildings or factories.

   o Example: INR 50,00,000 invested in acquiring a new office building.

3. **Vehicle Purchase:** Buying vehicles for business operations.

   o Example: INR 10,00,000 spent on purchasing delivery vehicles.

4. **Renovation of Buildings:** Major improvements or expansions to existing facilities.

   o Example: INR 20,00,000 spent on renovating the factory premises.

Illustration of Capital Expenditure:

The same furniture manufacturing SME spends INR 5,00,000 to buy a new piece of machinery that will be used for the next 10 years. This INR 5,00,000 is a capital expenditure because the machinery will provide long-term benefits and enhance the company's production capacity.

Distinguishing Between Revenue and Capital Expenditure

To avoid mistakes, accountants should ask the following questions:

1. **Duration of Benefit:** Will the expenditure provide a benefit for more than one accounting period?

2. **Nature of Expense:** Is the expense recurring (like monthly salaries) or one-time (like purchasing machinery)?

3. **Purpose:** Is the expenditure for maintaining current operations or for acquiring/improving a long-term asset?

Importance of Correct Classification

1. **Financial Accuracy:** Proper classification ensures accurate financial statements, reflecting the true financial position and performance of the business.

2. **Tax Implications:** Misclassifying expenses can lead to incorrect tax calculations. Capital expenditures are not fully deductible in the year incurred; they are depreciated over time. In contrast, revenue expenditures are fully deductible.

3. **Decision Making:** Accurate financial records help management make informed decisions regarding budgeting, investing, and strategic planning.

By maintaining clarity in distinguishing between revenue and capital expenditures, accountants can ensure that financial statements accurately reflect the company's financial health and comply with accounting standards.

Comparison

Aspect	Revenue Expenditure	Capital Expenditure
Definition	Costs incurred in the normal course of business operations to maintain or generate income within the current accounting period.	Funds used to acquire, upgrade, or maintain long-term assets expected to provide benefits over multiple accounting periods
Duration of Benefit	Short-term (within one accounting period)	Long-term (more than one accounting period)
Nature of Expense	Recurrent and regular expenses	Involves large one-time expenditures
Purpose	Maintain current operations	Acquire or improve long-term assets
Recorded on	Income statement as expenses	Balance sheet as assets, depreciated over time
Examples	Salaries, Rent, Utilities, Maintenance	Machinery purchase, Building acquisition, Vehicle purchase, Renovation

7.3   Expenses and Advances (assets)

Understanding the distinction between expenses and advances in accounting is crucial for accurately maintaining financial records. Here's a detailed explanation, including practical examples relevant to the Indian context and their respective accounting entries:

Distinction Between Expenses and Advances

Expenses

Expenses are costs incurred by a business in the process of earning revenue. They are recognized immediately and recorded in the profit and loss account.

Advances

Advances are payments made in anticipation of receiving goods, services, or for other purposes, which are yet to be fulfilled. They are recorded as assets until the related goods or services are received.

Practical Examples and Accounting Entries

1. **Advance Payment for Goods/Services**
   Scenario: An SME pays INR 50,000 in advance to a supplier for raw materials.

   Entry at the time of advance payment:
   Dr. Advance to Supplier Account (Assets)   50,000
   Cr. Bank Account   50,000

   Entry when goods are received:
   Dr. Raw Material Purchase Account (Expense)   50,000
   Cr. Advance to Supplier Account   50,000

2. **Advance Payment for Services**
   Scenario: An SME pays INR 30,000 in advance for advertising services to be received in the next month.

   Entry at the time of advance payment:
   Dr. Advance to Service Provider Account (Asset)   30,000
   Cr. Bank Account   30,000

   Entry when the advertising services are received:
   Dr. Advertising Expense Account (Expense)   30,000
   Cr. Advance to Service Provider Account (Asset)   30,000

Advances as Loans

Advances can also be in the nature of loans, which are expected to be repaid in the future and not necessarily for purchasing goods or receiving services.

1. **Loan to Employee**
   Scenario: An SME provides an advance of INR 20,000 to an employee, which will be deducted from their salary over the next four months.

Entry at the time of giving the advance:
Dr. Loan to Employee Account (Asset)   20,000
Cr. Bank Account   20,000

Entry when deducting the loan from salary (assuming monthly salary is INR 10,000 and deduction is INR 5,000 per month):
Dr. Salary Expense Account (Expense)   10,000
Cr. Bank Account   5,000
Cr. Loan to Employee Account   5,000

2. **Loan to Supplier**
   Scenario: An SME provides a loan of INR 100,000 to a supplier to help them in business, which will be repaid in installments over the next year.

   Entry at the time of giving the loan:
   Dr. Loan to Supplier Account (Asset)   100,000
   Cr. Bank Account   100,000

   Entry when receiving the repayment (assuming monthly repayment of INR 10,000):
   Dr. Bank Account   10,000
   Cr. Loan to Supplier Account   10,000

Key Points to Remember

- **Timing and Purpose**: If the payment is for an immediate expense, it should be recognized as an expense. If it's for a future benefit (goods/services yet to be received), it's an advance.

- **Nature of Payment**: Advances can be operational (for goods/services) or non-operational (loans to employees/suppliers).

- **Classification**: Advances are typically classified as current assets unless they are not expected to be settled within the normal operating cycle.

Properly distinguishing between expenses and advances ensures accurate financial reporting, aids in proper cash flow management, and complies with accounting principles.

7.4   Income Vs. Advance (liability)

In accounting, distinguishing between income and advances is crucial to accurately represent the financial health of a business. For Indian SMEs (Small and Medium Enterprises), this distinction can sometimes be confusing. Here's a detailed guide on how to differentiate between the two, along with practical examples relevant to the Indian context.

Income vs. Advances: Key Differences

1.   **Income**:

     o   Income represents amounts earned by the business from its core activities such as selling goods or rendering services.

     o   It is recorded in the income statement and impacts the profit and loss of the business.

     o   Income recognition is based on the principle of accrual accounting, which means it is recognized when earned, not necessarily when cash is received.

2.   **Advances**:

     o   Advances are amounts received by the business before the goods are delivered or services are rendered.

     o   They are recorded as liabilities on the balance sheet until the goods or services are provided.

     o   Advances do not impact the profit and loss statement until the corresponding goods/services are delivered/rendered.

Practical Examples

Example 1: Goods Sold with Advance Payment

Scenario: A manufacturing SME receives ₹1,00,000 as an advance from a retailer for the future delivery of goods.

Accounting Treatment:

- When advance is received:

    - **Debit**: Bank Account ₹1,00,000

    - **Credit**: Advances from Customers (Liability) ₹1,00,000

- When goods are delivered worth ₹1,00,000:

    - **Debit**: Advances from Customers (Liability) ₹1,00,000

    - **Credit**: Sales Revenue (Income) ₹1,00,000

Until the goods are delivered, the ₹1,00,000 remains as a liability and is not recognized as income.

Example 2: Service Rendered with Advance Payment

Scenario: A consultancy firm receives ₹50,000 in advance for a project that will be completed in three months.

Accounting Treatment:

- When advance is received:

    - **Debit**: Bank Account ₹50,000

    - **Credit**: Advances from Customers (Liability) ₹50,000

- As the service is rendered over three months, income is recognized proportionally. If the service value for one month is ₹16,667:

    - **Debit**: Advances from Customers (Liability) ₹16,667

    - **Credit**: Service Revenue (Income) ₹16,667

After three months, the entire advance would have been recognized as income.

Advances in the Nature of Loans

Example 3: Loan Received as Advance

Scenario: An SME receives ₹5,00,000 as an advance from an investor, which is actually a loan to be repaid in the future.

Accounting Treatment:

- When loan advance is received:

    - **Debit**: Bank Account ₹5,00,000

    - **Credit**: Loan from Investor (Liability) ₹5,00,000

- When the loan is repaid (let's say ₹1,00,000 is repaid after some time):

    - **Debit**: Loan from Investor (Liability) ₹1,00,000

    - **Credit**: Bank Account ₹1,00,000

This advance is purely a financial liability and does not affect the income statement.

7.5 Important Points to Remember

1. **Documentation**: Proper documentation should be maintained to differentiate between advance for goods/services and loan advances. Contracts, invoices, and agreements play a crucial role.

2. **Nature of Transaction**: Understand the nature of the transaction clearly. Is it for goods/services, or is it a financial advance/loan?

3. **Accrual Basis of Accounting**: Ensure to follow the accrual basis, where income is recognized when earned and not necessarily when received.

Conclusion

Understanding and correctly classifying income and advances is fundamental to accurate accounting. Advances for goods or services remain liabilities until the goods are delivered or services are rendered, whereas income is recognized in the income statement. Advances in the form of loans are treated as liabilities and do not affect the income statement until repaid. Proper documentation and clarity on the nature of transactions will aid in maintaining accurate financial records.

* * *

Chapter Challenge: Test Your Understanding with MCQs

1. **Which accounting method records revenues and expenses when they are actually received or paid?**

   (A) Cash accounting

   (B) Accrual accounting

   (C) Both

   (D) None

2. **Which method provides a more accurate financial picture of a company's performance?**

   (A) Cash accounting

   (B) Accrual accounting

   (C) Both provide the same accuracy

   (D) Neither

3. **How does the accrual method recognize expenses?**

   (A) When cash is paid

   (B) When the obligation is incurred

   (C) When the invoice is received

   (D) When cash is received

4. **What is the main difference between cash and accrual accounting?**

   (A) Timing of revenue recognition

   (B) Complexity of financial reporting

   (C) Requirement by regulatory bodies

   (D) None of the above

5. **Which of the following is characteristic of Revenue Expenditure?**

   (A) Short-term benefit

   (B) Long-term benefit

   (C) Involves large sums of money

   (D) Adds value to the business

6. **Which of the following is an example of Capital Expenditure?**

   (A) Salaries and Wages

   (B) Rent and Utilities

   (C) Purchase of Machinery

   (D) Maintenance and Repairs

7. **What distinguishes Capital Expenditure from Revenue Expenditure?**

   (A) Recurrent and regular expenses

   (B) Short-term benefit

   (C) Involves large sums of money

   (D) Recorded on the income statement as expenses

8. **Which statement is true regarding Revenue Expenditure?**

   (A) It is recorded on the balance sheet as assets.

   (B) It involves large one-time expenditures.

   (C) It is fully deductible in the year incurred.

   (D) It provides benefits over multiple accounting periods.

9. **Which of the following best describes an expense in accounting?**

   (A) Costs incurred in anticipation of future benefits.

   (B) Payments made for goods or services yet to be received.

   (C) Costs incurred by a business in the process of earning revenue.

   (D) Advances made to suppliers for future purchases.

10. What is the accounting treatment when an SME pays INR 50,000 in advance to a supplier for raw materials?

(A) Dr. Raw Material Purchase Account (Expense) 50,000, Cr. Advance to Supplier Account 50,000

(B) Dr. Advance to Supplier Account (Assets) 50,000, Cr. Bank Account 50,000

(C) Dr. Bank Account 50,000, Cr. Raw Material Purchase Account (Expense) 50,000

(D) Dr. Advance to Supplier Account (Assets) 50,000, Cr. Raw Material Purchase Account (Expense) 50,000

11. When does income get recognized in accounting?

(A) When cash is received.

(B) When goods or services are delivered.

(C) When earned, regardless of when cash is received.

(D) When expenses are incurred.

12. How are advances recorded in accounting until the corresponding goods/services are provided?

(A) As income in the income statement.

(B) As assets on the balance sheet.

(C) As liabilities on the balance sheet.

(D) As expenses in the profit and loss account.

Answers:

1.(A),	2.(B),	3.(B),	4.(A),	5(A),	6.(C),
7.(C),	8.(C),	9.(C),	10.(B),	11.(C),	12.(C)

CHAPTER 08

DECODING DEPRECIATION: BOOSTING YOUR BOTTOM LINE

Imagine you have a brand-new bicycle. When you first get it, it's shiny and new, and it's worth a lot. But as time goes by, the bicycle gets old, and parts might start to wear out. Maybe the tires get a little flat or the paint starts to chip. Because of this, the bicycle isn't worth as much as it was when it was new. This decrease in value over time is called depreciation.

8.1 Why Do Things Depreciate?

Things like bicycles, computers, and even cars depreciate because they get used, and as they get older, they aren't as good as they were when they were new. Just like people can get tired after a lot of play, objects can wear out after a lot of use.

8.2 How Does Depreciation Work in Business?

In a business, people buy things to help them make money. These things can be machines, computers, or even buildings. Just like your bicycle, these things lose value over time. Businesses need to keep track of how much value these items lose each year. This helps them know how much their things are worth at any time.

8.3   A Simple Example of Depreciation

Let's say a small business buys a computer for Rs. 50000. The business expects to use the computer for 5 years before it gets too old and slow. To find out how much the computer depreciates each year, the business can divide the cost of the computer by the number of years it will be used.

So, Rs. 50000 (cost of the computer) ÷ 5 years = Rs. 10000 per year.

This means the computer depreciates by Rs. 10000 each year. After the first year, the computer is worth Rs. 40000, after the second year, it's worth Rs. 30000, and so on, until after 5 years, it's worth Rs. 0 (for accounting purposes, even if it still works).

Why is Depreciation Important for a Business?

1. **Knowing the Real Value:** Businesses need to know how much their things are really worth, not just what they paid for them.

2. **Tax Benefits:** Sometimes, businesses can use depreciation to pay less in taxes. By showing that their things are losing value, they might be able to reduce their taxable income.

3. **Planning for the Future:** If a business knows when its things will be too old to use, it can plan to save money to buy new ones.

8.4   Different Ways to Calculate Depreciation

1. **Straight-Line Depreciation:** This is like our bicycle example. The value is spread out evenly over the years.
   Example:

   Let's say a small business buys a computer for Rs. 50000. The business expects to use the computer for 5 years before it gets too old and slow. To find out how much the computer depreciates each year, the business can divide the cost of the computer by the number of years it will be used.

   So, Rs. 50000 (cost of the computer) ÷ 5 years = Rs. 10000 per year.

This means the computer depreciates by Rs. 10000 each year. After the first year, the computer is worth Rs. 40000, after the second year, it's worth Rs. 30000, and so on, until after 5 years, it's worth Rs. 0 (for accounting purposes, even if it still works).

2. **Written Down Value Depreciation:** The Written Down Value (WDV) method, also known as the declining balance method, is another way to calculate depreciation. Unlike the straight-line method, where the same amount is depreciated each year, the WDV method applies a constant depreciation rate to the remaining value of the asset each year.

Example:

To illustrate the WDV method using the same example of a computer bought for Rs. 50000, let's assume an annual depreciation rate of 40%.

Here's how it works:

a. **First Year:**

   o   Initial Value: Rs. 50000

   o   Depreciation for the First Year = Rs. 50000 * 40% = Rs. 20000

   o   Value at the End of First Year = Rs. 50000 - Rs. 20000 = Rs. 30000

b. **Second Year:**

   o   Value at the Beginning of Second Year: Rs. 30000

   o   Depreciation for the Second Year = Rs. 30000 * 40% = Rs. 12000

   o   Value at the End of Second Year = Rs. 30000 - Rs. 12000 = Rs. 18000

c. Third Year:

- o Value at the Beginning of Third Year: Rs. 18000
- o Depreciation for the Third Year = Rs. 18000 * 40% = Rs. 7200
- o Value at the End of Third Year = Rs. 18000 - Rs. 7200 = Rs. 10800

d. Fourth Year:

- o Value at the Beginning of Fourth Year: Rs. 10800
- o Depreciation for the Fourth Year = Rs. 10800 * 40% = Rs. 4320
- o Value at the End of Fourth Year = Rs. 10800 - Rs. 4320 = Rs. 6480

e. Fifth Year:

- o Value at the Beginning of Fifth Year: Rs. 6480
- o Depreciation for the Fifth Year = Rs. 6480 * 40% = Rs. 2592
- o Value at the End of Fifth Year = Rs. 6480 - Rs. 2592 = Rs. 3888

Using the WDV method, the computer doesn't depreciate to Rs. 0 by the end of the 5 years. Instead, it continues to retain some residual value. The depreciation expense decreases each year since it's based on the diminishing value of the asset. This method is more reflective of how assets lose value more rapidly in the earlier years of their use.

Conclusion

Depreciation is a simple way of spreading out the cost of an item over its useful life. Just like your bicycle gets older and less valuable each year, the things businesses buy also lose value over time. Understanding depreciation helps businesses keep track of their real value, save on taxes, and plan for future expenses.

By thinking of depreciation like the aging of a bicycle, it becomes easier to understand how businesses manage the value of their assets over time.

* * *

Chapter Challenge: Test Your Understanding with MCQs

1. **Which of the following best describes depreciation?**

    (A) Increase in value over time

    (B) Constant value over time

    (C) Decrease in value over time

    (D) Fluctuating value over time

2. **Why do objects like bicycles and computers depreciate?**

    (A) Due to increase in quality with age

    (B) Due to limited use over time

    (C) Because they get worn out with use

    (D) Because they are replaced frequently

3. **What is one reason why depreciation is important for businesses?**

    (A) To know the real value of assets

    (B) To overstate the value of assets

    (C) To increase the taxable income

    (D) To complicate financial planning

4. Which depreciation method spreads the depreciation value evenly over the years?

(A) Written Down Value Depreciation

(B) Declining Balance Method

(C) Straight-Line Depreciation

(D) Accelerated Depreciation

5. In the Written Down Value (WDV) method, what happens to the depreciation amount over the years?

(A) It decreases gradually

(B) It increases gradually

(C) It remains constant

(D) It fluctuates unpredictably

Answers

1.(C), 2.(C), 3.(A), 4.(C), 5.(A)

UNLOCKING THE POWER OF ACCOUNTING VOUCHERS

Accounting vouchers play a critical role in the accounting process of any business or organization. They are documentary evidence of business transactions and provide a formal means of recording and summarizing financial activities. Here's an overview of accounting vouchers and their importance, along with examples of different types of vouchers like journal vouchers and cash vouchers:

9.1 Roles of Accounting Vouchers:

1. **Documentation of Transactions:** Vouchers serve as documentary evidence of financial transactions. They provide a written record of every financial event, which is crucial for maintaining transparency and accountability.

2. **Authorization and Approval:** Vouchers often require authorization or approval from designated personnel before transactions are recorded. This helps ensure that transactions are legitimate and properly authorized.

3. **Recording in Books of Accounts:** Vouchers are used to record transactions in the books of accounts. They provide the necessary details that enable accurate entry of transactions into the accounting system.

4. **Verification and Audit:** Vouchers serve as supporting documents during internal audits or external scrutiny. They help in verifying the accuracy and completeness of financial records.

5. **Financial Control:** Vouchers facilitate financial control by ensuring that transactions are properly documented and approved before they are processed.

Importance of Different Types of Accounting Vouchers:

Receipt Voucher

A **receipt voucher** is a document used to acknowledge the receipt of cash or funds from various sources. It is used to record cash inflows and serves as evidence that money has been received.

Key Features:

- **Date**: When the money was received.

- **Amount**: The total amount of money received.

- **Received From**: The individual or entity that provided the funds.

- **Purpose**: The reason for the receipt of funds (e.g., sales, loan repayment, investment, etc.).

- **Signature**: Authorized signatories acknowledging the receipt.

Uses:

- To document and verify incoming cash transactions.

- To support entries in the cash book or accounting system.

Payment Voucher

A **payment voucher** is a document used to authorize and record the payment of funds. It provides evidence of cash outflows and ensures that all payments are properly accounted for.

Key Features:

- **Date**: When the payment is made.

- **Amount**: The total amount of money paid.

- **Paid To**: The individual or entity receiving the payment.

- **Purpose**: The reason for the payment (e.g., payment of bills, salaries, purchase of goods, etc.).

- **Supporting Documents**: Attached invoices, bills, or receipts justifying the payment.

- **Signature**: Authorized signatories approving the payment.

Uses:

- To document and verify outgoing cash transactions.

- To support entries in the cash book or accounting system.

Journal Voucher

A **journal voucher** is a document used to record non-cash transactions in the accounting system. It is primarily used for adjusting entries, corrections, and internal transactions that do not involve immediate cash flows.

Key Features:

- **Date**: When the transaction is recorded.

- **Details of Transaction**: Description of the transaction, including accounts affected, debit and credit amounts.

- **Reason for Entry**: Explanation of why the entry is made (e.g., depreciation, accruals, error corrections).

- **Supporting Documentation**: Any documents that support the transaction.

- **Approval**: Authorized signatures for validation.

Uses:

- To record adjustments, corrections, and non-cash transactions.

- To ensure that all financial records are accurate and up-to-date.

Summary

- **Receipt Voucher**: Acknowledges receipt of cash; used for recording cash inflows.

- **Payment Voucher**: Authorizes and records cash payments; used for recording cash outflows.

- **Journal Voucher**: Records non-cash transactions; used for adjustments and corrections in financial records.

These sample vouchers are essential tools for maintaining accurate and reliable financial records, ensuring transparency, and facilitating the auditing process. Apart from the above-mentioned vouchers readers may other vouchers as may be required for their business such as Purchase Voucher, Separate Cash Payment & Bank Payment Voucher etc.

* * *

9.2 Sample Formats

9.2.1 Receipt Voucher:

<table>
<tr><td colspan="4" align="center">ABC & Co.</td><td rowspan="3" align="center">Original/
Duplicate</td></tr>
<tr><td align="center">Company
Logo</td><td colspan="3">Address: (Line 1)...</td></tr>
<tr><td></td><td colspan="3">Address: (Line 2)...</td></tr>
<tr><td colspan="5" align="center">Receipt Voucher</td></tr>
<tr><td>Voucher
Number:</td><td></td><td>Voucher
Date:</td><td></td><td>Amount
(Rs.)</td></tr>
<tr><td colspan="4">Debit (Mode of Receipt): Cash/ Bank</td><td></td></tr>
<tr><td colspan="4" align="center">If Received in Bank</td><td rowspan="3"></td></tr>
<tr><td colspan="2">Bank Name:</td><td>Cheque No.</td><td>Date:</td></tr>
<tr><td colspan="4">Narration:</td></tr>
<tr><td colspan="4">Credit Head (Received from):</td><td></td></tr>
<tr><td colspan="5">Against: Bill No. & Date/ Advance/ On Account</td></tr>
<tr><td>Prepared By</td><td>Received By</td><td>Checked By</td><td>Approved By</td><td>Entered By</td></tr>
<tr><td></td><td></td><td></td><td></td><td></td></tr>
</table>

9.2.2 Payment Voucher (simple)

<table>
<tr><td colspan="6" align="center">ABC & Co.</td></tr>
<tr><td>Company
Logo</td><td colspan="5">Address: (Line 1)..</td></tr>
<tr><td></td><td colspan="5">Address: (Line 2)..</td></tr>
<tr><td colspan="6"></td></tr>
<tr><td colspan="6" align="center">Payment Voucher</td></tr>
<tr><td colspan="6"></td></tr>
<tr><td>Voucher Number:</td><td></td><td>Voucher Date:</td><td></td><td></td><td>Amount (Rs.)</td></tr>
<tr><td colspan="5">Debit Head (Payment to):</td><td></td></tr>
<tr><td colspan="5">Against Bill No. & Date/ Advance/ On Account:</td><td></td></tr>
<tr><td colspan="5">Narration:</td><td></td></tr>
<tr><td colspan="5">Credit (Mode of Payment): Cash/ Bank</td><td></td></tr>
<tr><td colspan="6">Against: Bill No. & Date/ Advance/ On Account</td></tr>
<tr><td>If Paid by through Bank--></td><td></td><td>Bank Name</td><td>Date</td><td>Cheque No.</td><td></td></tr>
<tr><td></td><td></td><td></td><td></td><td></td><td></td></tr>
<tr><td colspan="6"></td></tr>
<tr><td>Prepared By</td><td>Checked by</td><td colspan="2">Approved By</td><td>Received By</td><td>Entered By</td></tr>
<tr><td></td><td></td><td colspan="2"></td><td></td><td></td></tr>
</table>

9.2.3 Payment Vouncher (with Calculation)

	ABC & Co.		
Company Logo	Address: (Line 1)... Address: (Line 2)...		

		Payment Voucher		
Voucher Number:		**Voucher Date:**		**Amount (Rs.)**
Debit Head (Payment to):				
Against Bill No. & Date/ Advance/ On Account:				
Narration:				
Credit (Mode of Payment): Cash/ Bank				

If Paid by through Bank--> RTGS/NEFT	**Bank Name**	**Date**	**Cheque No.**	

Payment Calculation:	Note	Amount (Rs.)
Bill Value (Before Tax):	A	
Add: CGST + SGST or IGST	B	
Add: Any Other Item in Bill (Mention Detail)	C	
Total Bill Value	**D= A + B + C**	
Less: Debit Note (If Any)	E	
Less: Income Tax TDS (If Any)	F	
Less: Any other Deduction from Bill (Mention Detail)	G	
Net Amount Payable	**H = D - E - F- G**	

Prepared By	Checked by	Approved By	Received By	Entered By

9.2.4 Journal Voucher

Company Logo	ABC & Co.	
	Address: (Line 1)...	
	Address: (Line 2)..	

<table>
<tr><td colspan="3" align="center">Journal Voucher</td></tr>
<tr><td colspan="3"></td></tr>
<tr><td>Voucher Number:</td><td>Voucher Date:</td><td>Amount (Rs.)</td></tr>
<tr><td colspan="2">Debit Head (Ledger Name):</td><td></td></tr>
<tr><td colspan="2">Narration:</td><td></td></tr>
<tr><td colspan="2">Credit Head (Ledger Name):</td><td></td></tr>
<tr><td colspan="2"></td><td></td></tr>
<tr><td colspan="3"></td></tr>
</table>

Prepared By	Checked by	Approved By	Entered By

Chapter Challenge: Test Your Understanding with MCQs

1. **What is the primary purpose of a payment voucher?**

   (A) To acknowledge the receipt of funds

   (B) To authorize and record cash payments

   (C) To document non-cash transactions

   (D) To prepare financial statements

2. **What supporting documents might be attached to a payment voucher?**

   (A) Bank statements

   (B) Sales invoices

   (C) Bills and receipts justifying the payment

   (D) Depreciation schedules

3. **Why is it important to have a payment voucher for every transaction?**

   (A) To replace the need for bank statements

   (B) To document and verify outgoing cash transactions

   (C) To ensure non-cash transactions are recorded

   (D) To avoid recording the purpose of payments

4. **What is the main function of an accounting voucher?**

   (A) To eliminate the need for bookkeeping

   (B) To provide documentary evidence of business transactions

   (C) To forecast future financial performance

   (D) To replace financial statements

5. Which type of voucher is used to record cash inflows?

(A) Payment Voucher

(B) Receipt Voucher

(C) Journal Voucher

(D) Purchase Voucher

6. Which voucher is used to record non-cash transactions and adjustments?

(A) Receipt Voucher

(B) Payment Voucher

(C) Journal Voucher

(D) Bank Voucher

7. Why is authorization important for accounting vouchers?

(A) To reduce the number of transactions

(B) To ensure transactions are legitimate and properly approved

(C) To increase transaction volume

(D) To avoid documenting transactions

Answers

1.(B),   2.(C).   3.(B),   4.(B),   5.(B),

6.(C),   7.(B).

BUDGETING UNLEASHED: PATHWAY TO PROSPERITY

Budgeting is the process of creating a financial plan for a specific period, typically a year. This plan outlines expected revenues, expenses, and other financial activities. In accounting terms, budgeting involves forecasting future financial performance and setting targets based on these projections. It serves as a guideline for managing resources, monitoring performance, and making informed financial decisions.

10.1　Why Budgeting is Essential in Accounting Terms

1.　**Financial Planning and Control**:

- ○ **Revenue Forecasting**: Helps in predicting future income, which is crucial for planning operations and ensuring the business can cover its costs.

- ○ **Expense Management**: Allows businesses to allocate funds to various departments and activities, ensuring that spending aligns with the company's financial goals.

- ○ **Cash Flow Management**: Ensures that the company can meet its financial obligations by projecting cash inflows and outflows.

2.　**Performance Measurement**:

- ○ **Setting Benchmarks**: Establishes financial targets and benchmarks against which actual performance can be measured.

- ○ **Variance Analysis**: Identifies deviations from the budget, allowing management to understand why these variances occurred and take corrective actions.

3.　**Strategic Planning**:

- ○ **Resource Allocation**: Ensures that resources are allocated efficiently to the most critical areas of the business, supporting strategic objectives.

- ○ **Risk Management**: Helps in identifying potential financial risks and creating strategies to mitigate them.

4.　**Operational Efficiency**:

- ○ **Coordination and Communication**: Encourages departments to communicate and coordinate, ensuring that all parts of the organization are aligned with the financial plan.

- ○ **Decision Making**: Provides a framework for making informed operational and strategic decisions based on financial data.

5. **Stakeholder Assurance**:

   o **Transparency**: Demonstrates to stakeholders, including investors, creditors, and regulatory bodies, that the company is financially responsible and has a plan to achieve its financial goals.

   o **Accountability**: Holds management accountable for financial performance, ensuring that they are managing the company's resources effectively.

10.2   Steps to Create a Budget

1. **Set Objectives and Goals**:

   o **Identify Financial Goals**: Determine what the organization aims to achieve in the upcoming period, such as increasing revenue, reducing costs, or investing in new projects.

   o **Define Objectives**: Set specific, measurable objectives that support the financial goals.

2. **Gather Historical Data**:

   o **Review Past Performance**: Analyse financial statements, past budgets, and historical data to understand trends and patterns.

   o **Identify Key Metrics**: Focus on critical metrics such as sales growth, expense ratios, and profit margins.

3. **Forecast Revenues**:

   o **Market Analysis**: Conduct market research to understand potential sales, considering factors like economic conditions, competition, and market demand.

   o **Sales Projections**: Estimate future sales based on historical data, market trends, and business strategies.

4. **Estimate Expenses**:

- o **Fixed Costs**: Identify fixed expenses such as rent, salaries, and insurance that remain constant regardless of business activity.

- o **Variable Costs**: Estimate variable expenses like raw materials, utilities, and commissions that fluctuate with business volume.

- o **Operational Costs**: Include costs associated with daily operations, such as marketing, travel, and administrative expenses.

5. **Develop Individual Budgets**:

- o **Departmental Budgets**: Each department (e.g., marketing, production, sales) creates its own budget based on expected activities and goals.

- o **Project Budgets**: For specific projects, create detailed budgets outlining all expected costs and revenues.

6. **Prepare Capital Expenditure Budget**:

- o **Identify Capital Needs**: Plan for major investments in long-term assets such as equipment, technology, and infrastructure.

- o **Prioritize Investments**: Determine the priority of capital projects based on strategic importance and financial impact.

7. **Create Cash Flow Budget**:

- o **Cash Inflows**: Project cash receipts from sales, loans, and other income sources.

- o **Cash Outflows**: Estimate cash payments for expenses, loan repayments, and capital expenditures.

- o **Liquidity Management**: Ensure that there is sufficient cash flow to meet financial obligations and avoid liquidity issues.

8. **Consolidate into Master Budget**:

   o **Integration**: Combine all individual budgets (departmental, project, capital expenditure, and cash flow) into a comprehensive master budget.

   o **Reconciliation**: Ensure that all parts of the budget align and that there are no discrepancies or overlaps.

9. **Review and Approve**:

   o **Management Review**: Present the draft budget to senior management/ qualified professional for reveiw and feedback.

   o **Adjustments**: Make necessary adjustments based on feedback and further analysis.

   o **Approval**: Obtain final approval from top management or the board of directors.

10. **Implementation and Monitoring**:

   o **Communicate the Budget**: Distribute the approved budget to all relevant departments, teams and stakeholders.

   o **Monitoring**: Regularly track actual performance against the budget to identify variances.

   o **Variance Analysis**: Analyze significant variances to understand the causes and take corrective actions.

   o **Adjustments**: Make mid-period adjustments to the budget if necessary, based on changes in business conditions or unforeseen events.

A draft of Budget for the coming years is presented herein below by taking forward to the same financial statement as discussed earlier under the Chapter 5 "Understanding the Financial Statement"

10.3 Sample Format

ABC & CO.
ADDRESS:...........
Balance Sheet as at 31st March...................

Particulars	Note No	As at 31 March, 2023	As at 31st March 2024	As at 31st March 2025	As at 31st March 2026
					(Rs. In Lacs)
		Audited	Audited	Budgeted	Projected
I. EQUITY AND LIABILITIES					
(1) Shareholder's Funds					
(a) Share Capital	1	200.00	200.00	200.00	200.00
(b) Reserves and Surplus	2	60.00	89.50	129.75	214.25
(c) Money received against share warrants		0.00	0.00	0.00	0.00
(2) Share Application Money Pending Allotment		0.00	0.00	0.00	0.00
(3) Non-Current Liabilities					
(a) Long-term borrowings	3	200.00	180.00	150.00	350.00
(b) Deferred tax liabilities (Net)		0.00	0.00	0.00	0.00
(c) Other Long term liabilities		0.00	0.00	0.00	0.00
(d) Long term provisions		0.00	0.00	0.00	0.00
(4) Current Liabilities					
(a) Short-term borrowings	4	100.00	100.00	150.00	200.00
(b) Trade payables	5	25.00	40.00	50.00	60.00
(c) Other current liabilities	6	5.00	8.00	5.00	8.00
(d) Short-term provisions	7	8.75	11.50	15.75	30.50
TOTAL		**598.75**	**629.00**	**700.50**	**1062.75**

Particulars	Note No	As at 31 March, 2023	As at 31st March 2024	As at 31st March 2025	As at 31st March 2026 (Rs. In Lacs)
		Audited	Audited	Budgeted	Projected
II.ASSETS					
(1) Non-current assets					
(a) Fixed assets					
(i) Tangible assets	8	400.00	390.00	382.00	576.00
(ii) Intangible assets	9	3.00	3.00	3.00	3.00
(iii) Capital work-in-progress		0.00	0.00	0.00	0.00
(iv) Intangible assets under development		0.00	0.00	0.00	0.00
(b) Non-current investments	10	15.00	20.00	30.00	30.00
(c) Deferred tax assets (net)					
(d) Long term loans and advances	12	40.00	40.00	45.00	50.00
(e) Other non-current assets		0.00	0.00	0.00	0.00
(2) Current assets					
(a) Current investments		0.00	0.00	0.00	0.00
(b) Inventories	13	41.00	86.00	141.00	266.00
(c) Trade receivables	14	70.00	80.00	85.00	120.00
(d) Cash and cash equivalents	15	15.75	5.00	8.00	7.75
(e) Short-term loans and advances	16	14.00	3.50	4.50	7.00
(f) Other current assets	17	0.00	1.50	2.00	3.00
TOTAL		**598.75**	**629.00**	**700.50**	**1062.75**

ABC & CO.
ADDRESS:............
Profit and Loss statement for the year ended................

Particulars	Note No	Figures as at the end of 31st March 2023	Figures as at the end of 31st March 2024	Figures as at the end of 31st March 2025	(Rs. In Lacs) Figures as at the end of 31st March 2026
		Audited	Audited	Budgeted	Projected
I. Revenue from operations (Gross)	18	220.00	325.00	488.00	732.00
Less: Excise Duty		-	-	-	-
Revenue from operations (Net)		220.00	325.00	488.00	732.00
II. Other Income	19	0.00	0.00	0.00	0.00
III. Total Revenue (I +II)		**220.00**	**325.00**	**488.00**	**732.00**
IV. Expenses:					
Cost of materials consumed	20	0.00	0.00	0.00	0.00
Purchase of Stock-in-Trade	21	100.00	194.00	291.00	457.00
Changes in inventories of finished goods, work-in-progress and Stock-in-Trade	22	(30.00)	(45.00)	(55.00)	(125.00)
Employee benefit expense	23	40.00	45.00	68.00	98.00
Financial costs	24	25.00	30.00	45.00	68.00
Depreciation and amortization expense	25	12.00	10.00	8.00	10.00
Preliminary and Preoperative Exp.		0.00	0.00	0.00	0.00
Other expenses	26	38.00	45.00	68.00	102.00
Total Expenses		**185.00**	**279.00**	**425.00**	**610.00**
V. Profit before exceptional and extraordinary items and tax	(III - IV)	35.00	46.00	63.00	122.00
VI. Exceptional Items		0.00	0.00	0.00	0.00
VII. Profit before extraordinary items and tax (V + VI)		35.00	46.00	63.00	122.00
VIII. Extraordinary Items		0.00	0.00	0.00	0.00
IX. Profit before tax (VII + VIII)		**35.00**	**46.00**	**63.00**	**122.00**

Particulars	Note No	Figures as at the end of 31st March 2023	Figures as at the end of 31st March 2024	Figures as at the end of 31st March 2025	Figures as at the end of 31st March 2026 (Rs. In Lacs)
		Audited	Audited	Budgeted	Projected
X. Tax expense:					
(1) Current tax	27	8.75	11.50	15.75	30.50
(2) Deferred tax Liabilities (Assets)		0.00	0.00	0.00	0.00
XI. Profit (Loss) from the period from continuing operations	(IX + X))	26.25	34.50	47.25	91.50
XII. Profit/(Loss) from discontinuing operations		0.00	0.00	0.00	0.00
XIII. Tax expense of discounting operations		0.00	0.00	0.00	0.00
XIV. Profit/(Loss) from Discontinuing operations (XII - XIII)		0.00	0.00	0.00	0.00
XV. Profit/(Loss) for the period (XI + XIV)		**26.25**	**34.50**	**47.25**	**91.50**
XVI. Earning per equity share:					
(1) Basic		1.31	1.73	2.36	4.58
(2) Diluted		1.31	1.73	2.36	4.58

✳ ✳ ✳

Chapter Challenge: Test Your Understanding with MCQs

1. **Which of the following best describes budgeting in accounting terms?**

   (A) A process of tracking daily expenses.

   (B) A process of creating a financial plan for a specific period, typically a year.

   (C) A method of saving money on operational costs.

   (D) A technique for paying off debts faster.

2. **What is the primary purpose of revenue forecasting in budgeting?**

   (A) To increase the company's debt.

   (B) To plan for unexpected expenses.

   (C) To predict future income and ensure the business can cover its costs.

   (D) To reduce employee salaries.

3. **Which of the following is NOT a step in creating a budget?**

   (A) Set objectives and goals.

   (B) Ignore past performance data.

   (C) Forecast revenues.

   (D) Develop individual budgets.

4. **Why is variance analysis important in the budgeting process?**

   (A) To randomly change the budget.

   (B) To identify deviations from the budget and understand the causes.

   (C) To ignore discrepancies in financial performance.

   (D) To ensure fixed costs are always reduced.

5. **Which type of budget would be specifically created for major investments in long-term assets?**

    (A) Departmental budget

    (B) Cash flow budget

    (C) Project budget

    (D) Capital expenditure budget

6. **What is the final step in the budgeting process according to the provided steps?**

    (A) Forecasting revenues.

    (B) Gathering historical data.

    (C) Reviewing and approving the budget.

    (D) Implementing and monitoring the budget.

Answers

1.(B), 2.(C), 3.(B), 4.(B), 5.(D), 6.(D)

CASH IS KING: UNDERSTANDING CASH FLOW MANAGEMENT

As we all know that Cash is the blood of any business, we need to understand the effective cash flow management. It is the process of monitoring, analyzing, and optimizing the net amount of cash receipts minus cash expenses. For small and medium-sized enterprises (SMEs), effective cash flow management is crucial for several reasons:

1. **Business Survival**:

   o **Liquidity Maintenance**: Ensuring there is enough cash on hand to meet immediate and short-term obligations is critical for survival. Poor cash flow management can lead to insolvency, even if the business is profitable on paper.

   o **Operational Continuity**: Consistent cash flow enables the business to maintain day-to-day operations without disruption, such as paying salaries, suppliers, and utility bills.

2. **Decision Making**:

   o **Informed Decisions**: Understanding cash flow helps entrepreneurs make informed decisions regarding investments, expansions, and cost-cutting measures.

- o **Planning and Forecasting**: Accurate cash flow forecasts allow businesses to plan for future expenses and investments, helping avoid financial shortfalls.

3. **Cost Management**:

- o **Avoiding Debt**: Proper cash management helps in avoiding unnecessary borrowing and the associated interest costs.

- o **Negotiating Power**: With strong cash flow, SMEs can negotiate better terms with suppliers and potentially receive discounts for early payments.

4. **Growth and Expansion**:

- o **Investment Opportunities**: Positive cash flow provides the funds needed for expansion, new projects, and innovation without relying heavily on external funding.

- o **Market Position**: Consistent cash flow enhances the business's ability to respond quickly to market opportunities and threats.

5. **Risk Management**:

- o **Economic Downturns**: Adequate cash reserves act as a buffer during economic downturns, ensuring the business can weather periods of reduced revenue.

- o **Unexpected Expenses**: A healthy cash flow can cover unforeseen expenses, such as repairs or urgent supply needs.

11.1   How to Manage Cash Flow Effectively

1. **Regular Monitoring and Forecasting**:

- o **Cash Flow Statements**: Regularly prepare and review cash flow statements to track inflows and outflows. This helps identify patterns and predict future cash flow.

- o **Forecasting**: Create cash flow forecasts based on historical data and expected future activities. Update these forecasts frequently to reflect changing business conditions.

2. **Optimize Receivables**:

   o **Invoice Promptly**: Send out invoices as soon as goods or services are delivered. The quicker the invoice is sent, the sooner payment can be expected.

   o **Credit Terms**: Offer reasonable credit terms to customers and encourage early payments through discounts.

   o **Follow Up**: Implement a systematic follow-up process for overdue accounts to ensure timely collections.

3. **Control Payables**:

   o **Manage Expenses**: Keep a close eye on all expenses. Prioritize essential spending and look for cost-saving opportunities.

   o **Negotiate Terms**: Negotiate favorable payment terms with suppliers to delay outflows while maintaining good relationships.

   o **Utilize Payment Cycles**: Take advantage of full payment terms offered by suppliers, and pay on the due date rather than early, unless there's a discount for early payment.

4. **Maintain Cash Reserves**:

   o **Emergency Fund**: Set aside a portion of cash each month into a reserve fund to handle unexpected expenses or downturns.

   o **Buffer Cash**: Maintain a buffer of cash to cover at least three to six months of operating expenses.

5. **Optimize Inventory**:

   o **Inventory Management**: Avoid tying up too much cash in inventory. Use inventory management techniques like just-in-time (JIT) to reduce holding costs and improve cash flow.

   o **Inventory Turnover**: Regularly analyze inventory turnover rates to ensure optimal stock levels.

6. **Cost Control and Efficiency**:

   o **Budgeting**: Implement strict budgeting practices. Regularly review budgets and adjust them based on actual performance and changing circumstances.

- ○ **Cost Reduction**: Continuously seek ways to reduce costs without compromising quality. This can include negotiating better rates with suppliers, outsourcing non-core activities, and adopting technology to increase efficiency.

7. **Leverage Technology**:

   - ○ **Accounting Software**: Use accounting software to automate and streamline cash flow management processes. This can help track transactions in real-time, generate reports, and forecast future cash flow.

   - ○ **Payment Solutions**: Utilize digital payment solutions to facilitate quicker and more reliable transactions.

8. **Access to Financing**:

   - ○ **Credit Lines**: Establish lines of credit with banks to provide a safety net for times when cash flow is tight.

   - ○ **Short-term Loans**: Consider short-term loans or advances to manage cash flow gaps, but use them judiciously to avoid excessive debt.

9. **Regular Reviews and Adjustments**:

   - ○ **Periodic Reviews**: Regularly review cash flow performance and compare it with forecasts to identify variances. Investigate and address any significant discrepancies.

   - ○ **Adapt Strategies**: Be prepared to adapt cash flow strategies based on the business environment and operational changes.

By understanding the importance of cash flow management and implementing these strategies, SME entrepreneurs can ensure their businesses remain financially healthy and resilient in the face of challenges. Effective cash flow management is not just about keeping the business afloat; it's about enabling sustainable growth and long-term success. A draft format of tracking and analysing Cash flow is depicted below:

11.2 Sample Format

ABC & Co.

Address:
Monthly Cash Flow Projection

	Budget	M 1	M 2	M 3	M 4	M 5	M 6	M 7	M 8	M 9	M 10	M 11	M 12	Total
1. Cash on Hand [Beginning of month]		-	-	-	-	-	-	-	-	-	-	-	-	
2. Cash Receipts														
(a) Cash Sales														-
(b) Collections from Credit Accounts														-
(c) Loan or Other Cash Injection														-
3. Total Cash Receipts [2a + 2b + 2c=3]	-	-	-	-	-	-	-	-	-	-	-	-	-	-
4. Total Cash Available [Before cash out] (1 + 3)	-	-	-	-	-	-	-	-	-	-	-	-	-	
5. Cash Paid Out														
(a) Purchases (Merchandise)														-
(b) Gross Wages (ex. withdrawals)														-
(c) Payroll Expenses (Taxes, etc.)														-
(d) Outside Services														-
(e) Supplies (Office and operating)														-
(f) Repairs and Maintenance														-
(g) Advertising														-
(h) Auto, Delivery, and Travel														-
(i) Accounting and Legal														-
(j) Rent														-
(k) Telephone														-

	Budget	M 1	M 2	M 3	M 4	M 5	M 6	M 7	M 8	M 9	M 10	M 11	M 12	Total
(l) Utilities														-
(m) Insurance														-
(n) Taxes (Real Estate, etc.)														-
(o) Interest														-
(p) Other Expenses [Specify each]														-
(q) Miscellaneous [Unspecified]														-
(r) Subtotal	-	-	-	-	-	-	-	-	-	-	-	-	-	-
(s) Loan Principal Payment														-
(t) Capital Purchases [Specify]														-
(u) Other Start-up Costs														-
(v) Reserve and/or Escrow [Specify]														-
(w) Owner's Withdrawal														-
6. Total Cash Paid Out [Total 5a thru 5w]	-	-	-	-	-	-	-	-	-	-	-	-	-	-
7. CASH POSITION [End of month] (4 minus 6)	-	-	-	-	-	-	-	-	-	-	-	-	-	
Essential Operating Data [Non-cash flow information]														
A. Sales Volume [Rs.]														-
B. Accounts Rec. [End of Month]														
C. Bad Debt [End of Month]														-
D. Inventory on Hand [End of Month]														
E. Accounts Payable [End of Month]														
F. Depreciation														-

* * *

Chapter Challenge: Test Your Understanding with MCQs

1. **Why is liquidity maintenance critical for SMEs?**

   (A) It allows the business to earn more profits.

   (B) It ensures there is enough cash on hand to meet immediate and short-term obligations.

   (C) It helps in avoiding taxes.

   (D) It increases the value of the company's shares.

2. **How can SMEs use strong cash flow to their advantage with suppliers?**

   (A) By increasing the prices of their products.

   (B) By delaying payments indefinitely.

   (C) By negotiating better terms and potentially receiving discounts for early payments.

   (D) By reducing the quality of products.

3. **What is a key benefit of regular cash flow forecasting for SMEs?**

   (A) It helps the business avoid paying taxes.

   (B) It ensures compliance with government regulations.

   (C) It allows businesses to plan for future expenses and investments, helping avoid financial shortfalls.

   (D) It guarantees the business will always have a profit.

4. Which strategy can help SMEs optimize their receivables?

(A) Delay sending invoices to avoid early payments.

(B) Offer long-term credit terms without follow-ups.

(C) Send out invoices promptly and encourage early payments through discounts.

(D) Ignore overdue accounts.

5. What is the purpose of maintaining an emergency fund for SMEs?

(A) To invest in high-risk stocks.

(B) To cover unexpected expenses or economic downturns.

(C) To increase the salaries of executives.

(D) To expand the business rapidly without planning.

Answers

1.(B),   **2.**(C),   **3.**(C),   **4.**(C),   **5.**(B)

THE ART AND SCIENCE OF INVENTORY MANAGEMENT

12.1 Introduction to Inventory Management

Inventory management is the process of ordering, storing, and using a company's inventory. This includes the management of raw materials, components, and finished products, as well as warehousing and processing such items. Effective inventory management is crucial for ensuring a company can meet customer demand without incurring unnecessary costs.

12.2 Objectives of Inventory Management

The primary objectives of inventory management are:

1. **Ensuring Product Availability:** To maintain sufficient stock to meet customer demand.

2. **Optimizing Inventory Levels:** To minimize the costs associated with holding inventory.

3. **Efficient Inventory Tracking:** To accurately track inventory to prevent overstocking or stockouts.

4. **Minimizing Obsolescence:** To ensure products are sold before they become obsolete.

5. **Improving Cash Flow:** By balancing inventory costs and ensuring efficient use of capital.

12.3   Types of Inventory

1. **Raw Materials:** Basic materials used to produce goods.

2. **Work-In-Progress (WIP):** Semi-finished products that are still in the production process.

3. **Finished Goods:** Products that are ready for sale.

4. **MRO Goods (Maintenance, Repair, and Operations):** Items used to support the production process but not part of the final product.

5. **Traded Stock:** Goods purchased are sold as such

12.4   Inventory Management Techniques

1. **Just-In-Time (JIT):** Inventory system that aligns raw-material orders from suppliers directly with production schedules.

2. **ABC Analysis:** Inventory categorization technique where 'A' items are the most valuable, 'B' items are less valuable, and 'C' items are the least valuable.

3. **Economic Order Quantity (EOQ):** The optimal order quantity that minimizes the total inventory costs.

4. **Safety Stock:** Extra inventory kept to prevent stockouts caused by unpredictable demand.

5. **Perpetual Inventory System:** Continuous tracking of inventory levels using software.

6. **Periodic Inventory System:** Inventory counts conducted at regular intervals.

12.5 Inventory Management Metrics

1. **Inventory Turnover:** A ratio showing how many times a company's inventory is sold and replaced over a period.

2. **Days Sales of Inventory (DSI):** The average number of days it takes for inventory to be sold.

3. **Stockout Rate:** The frequency of inventory being out of stock.

4. **Carrying Cost of Inventory:** The total cost of holding inventory including storage, insurance, and taxes.

5. **Order Accuracy Rate:** The percentage of orders correctly filled and delivered on time.

12.6 Technologies in Inventory Management

1. **Barcode Systems:** Used to track inventory through scanning items at various stages.

2. **RFID (Radio Frequency Identification):** Uses electromagnetic fields to automatically identify and track tags attached to objects.

3. **Inventory Management Software:** Software solutions that provide real-time inventory tracking and reporting.

4. **Automated Warehousing:** Use of robots and automated systems to handle inventory storage and retrieval.

12.7 Inventory Management Best Practices

1. **Regular Audits:** Conduct regular inventory audits to ensure accuracy.

2. **Accurate Forecasting:** Use historical data and market analysis for demand forecasting.

3. **Supplier Relationships:** Develop strong relationships with suppliers for reliable inventory replenishment.

4. **Lean Inventory:** Focus on reducing waste and optimizing inventory levels.

5. **Cross-Functional Teams:** Collaborate across departments to ensure efficient inventory management.

12.8 Challenges in Inventory Management

1. **Demand Variability:** Unpredictable changes in customer demand.

2. **Supply Chain Disruptions:** Issues such as supplier delays or transportation problems.

3. **Inventory Accuracy:** Ensuring the accuracy of inventory data.

4. **Storage Constraints:** Limited storage space affecting inventory levels.

5. **Technological Integration:** Challenges in integrating new inventory management systems with existing processes.

Effective inventory management is critical for the smooth operation and profitability of any business. By implementing the right strategies and technologies, businesses can ensure they meet customer demand, optimize costs, and maintain accurate inventory records. The continuous evaluation and maintenance of proper stock records can lead to significant competitive advantages and contribute to overall business success.

To understand the suggested list of stock records to be maintained by an SME for effective inventory management, it's important to note that the maintenance of stock records by a trading entity is less complex compared to that of a manufacturing entity. For a broad understanding, let's consider the example of a bakery manufacturing unit and how it should maintain its stock records.

12.9 Suggested List of Stock Records To Be Maintained

1. **Inventory Records**

   o **Inventory Master List**: A comprehensive list of all items in stock, including raw materials, work-in-progress (WIP), and finished goods. This should include item names, descriptions, unit of measure, SKU numbers, and locations.

   o **Stock Levels**: Records of the quantities of each item currently in stock, including minimum and maximum stock levels to trigger reorders.

o **Stock Movements**: Logs of all stock movements, including receipts, issues, returns, and adjustments. This helps in tracking the flow of inventory in and out of storage.

2. **Purchase Records**

o **Requisition Slips:** As asked by the production/ stock maintenance team for procurement of material

o **Purchase Orders (POs)**: Documents detailing the items ordered from suppliers, including quantities, prices, and delivery dates.

o **Supplier Invoices**: Bills received from suppliers for goods purchased. These should be matched with POs and delivery receipts to ensure accuracy.

o **Goods Received Notes (GRNs)**: Records confirming the receipt of goods ordered, including the condition and quantity of items received.

3. **Production Records**

o **Production Orders**: Instructions for producing specific quantities of products, detailing the raw materials and processes required.

o **Bill of Materials (BOM)**: Lists of raw materials, components, and quantities needed to manufacture a product.

o **Work-in-Progress (WIP) Records**: Logs of items that are in the process of being produced but are not yet finished.

4. **Sales Records**

o **Sales Orders**: Documents detailing customer orders, including quantities, prices, and delivery dates.

o **Sales Invoices:** Bills issued to customers for goods sold. These should be matched with sales orders and delivery notes.

5. **Inventory Valuation Records**

   - **Costing Records**: Details of the costs associated with each item in inventory, including purchase costs, production costs, and overheads. This is essential for valuing inventory accurately.

   - **Periodic Inventory Reports**: Summaries of inventory values at specific intervals (e.g., monthly, quarterly). These reports are used for financial reporting and to assess stock levels and valuation over time.

6. **Adjustment Records**

   - **Stock Adjustment Logs**: Records of any adjustments made to stock levels due to errors, damage, spoilage, or theft. These logs should include reasons for adjustments and the personnel responsible.

7. **Waste and Spoilage Records**

   - **Waste Logs**: Details of any inventory that is wasted or spoiled, including quantities and reasons for spoilage. This helps in identifying patterns and taking corrective actions.

8. **Reconciliation Records**

   - **Physical Inventory Counts**: Regularly scheduled counts of physical inventory to compare with recorded stock levels. Discrepancies should be investigated and reconciled.

   - **Discrepancy Reports**: Detailed reports on any discrepancies found during physical counts, including explanations and corrective actions taken.

9. **Inventory Control Records**

   - **Reorder Point Logs**: Records indicating when stock levels reach a point that triggers a new order. This helps in maintaining adequate stock levels without overstocking.

   - **Safety Stock Levels**: Records of buffer stock maintained to prevent stockouts during unexpected demand or supply chain disruptions.

10. Financial Records

- **Inventory Turnover Reports**: Analysis of how frequently inventory is sold and replaced over a period. High turnover rates typically indicate good sales and efficient inventory management.

- **Aging Reports**: Reports showing the age of inventory items, helping to identify slow-moving or obsolete stock.

12.10   Format of Report for Stock Records

(Considering Example of a Bakery Unit)

1. Inventory Master List

Item Name	Description	Unit of Measure	SKU Number	Location
Flour	All-purpose flour	Kg	FLR001	Storage Room
Sugar	Granulated sugar	Kg	SGR002	Storage Room
Eggs	Fresh eggs	Trays	EGG003	Refrigerator
Butter	Unsalted butter	Kg	BTR004	Refrigerator
Chocolate	Dark chocolate	Kg	CHO005	Pantry

2. Stock Levels

Item Name	Current Stock	Minimum Stock Level	Maximum Stock Level	Reorder Point
Flour	150 kg	50 kg	300 kg	100 kg
Sugar	130 kg	30 kg	150 kg	50 kg
Eggs	8 trays	2 trays	20 trays	5 trays
Butter	53 kg	20 kg	100 kg	30 kg
Chocolate	10 kg	5 kg	50 kg	10 kg

3. Stock Movements

Date	Item Name	Quantity Received	Quantity Issued	Balance	Remarks
20-05-24	Flour	200 kg	50 kg	150 kg	Received new stock
20-05-24	Eggs	5 trays	2 trays	8 trays	Used for baking
20-05-24	Butter	10 kg	5 kg	53 kg	Production use

4. Purchase Orders (POs)

PO Number	Date	Supplier	Items	Quantities	Prices	Delivery Date	Remarks
2024-001	18-05-24	ABC Flour Supplies	Flour, Sugar	200 kg, 100 kg	Rs. 200, Rs. 100	2024-05-20	First order of the month
2024-002	20-05-24	Fresh Dairy Ltd	Eggs, Butter	10 trays, 20 kg	Rs. 50, Rs. 200	2024-05-21	Regular bi-weekly order

5. Supplier Invoices

Invoice Number	Date	Supplier	Items	Amount	PO Number
INV-2024-001	20-05-24	ABC Flour Supplies	Flour, Sugar	Rs. 300	2024-001
INV-2024-002	21-05-24	Fresh Dairy Ltd	Eggs, Butter	Rs. 250	2024-002

6. Goods Received Notes (GRNs)

GRN Number	Date	Supplier	Items	Quantities	Condition	PO Number	Remarks
GRN-2024-001	20-05-24	ABC Flour Supplies	Flour, Sugar	200 kg, 100 kg	Good	2024-001	Received complete order
GRN-2024-002	21-05-24	Fresh Dairy Ltd	Eggs, Butter	10 trays, 20 kg	Good	2024-002	Received in good condition

7. Production Orders

Production Order Number	Date	Product	Quantity	Raw Materials Required	Status
PO-2024-001	20-05-24	Bread	50 loaves	Flour, Sugar, Eggs	Completed
PO-2024-002	21-05-24	Cookies	200 pcs	Flour, Sugar, Butter	Completed

8. Bill of Materials (BOM)

Product	Raw Material	Quantity Required	Unit of Measure
Bread	Flour	1 kg per 10 loaves	kg
Bread	Sugar	0.2 kg per 10 loaves	kg
Bread	Eggs	1 tray per 50 loaves	trays
Cookies	Flour	0.5 kg per 50 pcs	Kg
Cookies	Sugar	0.25 kg per 50 pcs	Kg
Cookies	Butter	0.1 kg per 50 pcs	Kg

9. Work-in-Progress (WIP) Records

Date	Product	Stage	Quantity	Expected Completion
20-05-24	Bread	Dough Mixing	50 loaves	20-05-24
21-05-24	Cookies	Baking	200 pcs	21-05-24

10. Sales Orders

Sales Order Number	Date	Customer	Items Ordered	Quantities	Delivery Date	Status
SO-2024-001	19-05-24	John Doe	Bread	5 loaves	20-05-24	Delivered
SO-2024-002	20-05-24	Jane Smith	Cookies	50 pcs	21-05-24	Delivered

11. Sales Invoices

Invoice Number	Date	Customer	Items	Amount	Sales Order Number
SI-2024-001	20-05-24	John Doe	Bread	Rs. 25	SO-2024-001
SI-2024-002	21-05-24	Jane Smith	Cookies	Rs. 50	SO-2024-002

12. Inventory Valuation Records

Week Ending	Item Name	Opening Balance	Purchases	Usage	Spoiled	Closing Balance	Valuation
24-05-24	Butter	30 kg	50 kg	25 kg	2 kg	53 kg	Rs. 530

13. Stock Adjustment Logs

Date	Item Name	Adjustment Type	Quantity	New Balance	Reason	Personnel
22-05-24	Eggs	Spoilage	-1 tray	8 trays	Damaged during transport	Manager
23-05-24	Butter	Spoilage	-2 kg	53 kg	Expired	Inventory Clerk

14. Waste Logs

Date	Item Name	Quantity	Reason	Action Taken
22-05-24	Eggs	1 tray	Damaged during transport	Disposed
23-05-24	Butter	2 kg	Expired	Disposed

15. Physical Inventory Counts

Date	Item Name	Recorded Stock	Physical Count	Discrepancy	Comments
23-05-24	Flour	150 kg	148 kg	-2 kg	Minor spillage
23-05-24	Sugar	130 kg	130 kg	0	Accurate

16. Discrepancy Reports

Date	Item Name	Discrepancy	Reason	Corrective Action
23-05-24	Flour	-2 kg	Minor spillage	Training on handling

17. Reorder Point Logs

Item Name	Minimum Level	Current Level	Reorder Point	Action	Order Date
Eggs	2 trays	4 trays	5 trays	Order	22-05-24
Butter	20 kg	30 kg	30 kg	Order	21-05-24

18. Safety Stock Levels

Item Name	Safety Stock Level	Current Stock	Reorder Required?
Flour	50 kg	150 kg	No
Sugar	30 kg	130 kg	No

19. Inventory Turnover Reports

Month	Item Name	Opening Stock	Closing Stock	Sales	Inventory Turnover Ratio
May 2024	Flour	100 kg	150 kg	200 kg	1.33
May 2024	Sugar	50 kg	130 kg	120 kg	1.20

20. Aging Reports

Item Name	Date Purchased	Quantity	Age (days)	Status
Flour	10-05-24	100 kg	14	Fresh
Eggs	15-05-24	5 trays	9	Fresh
Butter	01-05-24	10 kg	23	Use soon

Note:

1. All the above formats are indicative only and can be easily managed through Accounting with Inventory software.

2. These formats will help ensure comprehensive and efficient inventory management for a small bakery, covering all necessary aspects from procurement to sales and waste management.

* * *

Chapter Challenge: Test Your Understanding with MCQs

1. **What is the primary objective of inventory management?**

   (A) Reducing employee turnover

   (B) Increasing the number of suppliers

   (C) Ensuring product availability

   (D) Maximizing warehouse space

2. **Which of the following is NOT a type of inventory?**

   (A) Raw Materials

   (B) Work-In-Progress (WIP)

   (C) Financial Reports

   (D) Finished Goods

3. **What inventory management technique involves aligning raw-material orders directly with production schedules?**

   (A) ABC Analysis

   (B) Economic Order Quantity (EOQ)

   (C) Safety Stock

   (D) Just-In-Time (JIT)

4. **Which inventory management metric shows how many times a company's inventory is sold and replaced over a period?**

   (A) Stockout Rate

   (B) Inventory Turnover

   (C) Carrying Cost of Inventory

   (D) Days Sales of Inventory (DSI)

5. **What technology uses electromagnetic fields to automatically identify and track tags attached to objects?**

(A) Barcode Systems

(B) RFID (Radio Frequency Identification)

(C) Automated Warehousing

(D) Perpetual Inventory System

6. **What type of inventory includes semi-finished products that are still in the production process?**

(A) Raw Materials

(B) Finished Goods

(C) Work-In-Progress (WIP)

(D) MRO Goods

7. **Which inventory record is a comprehensive list of all items in stock, including raw materials, WIP, and finished goods?**

(A) Stock Levels

(B) Inventory Master List

(C) Stock Movements

(D) Goods Received Notes (GRNs)

8. **What type of report helps identify slow-moving or obsolete stock?**

(A) Inventory Turnover Reports

(B) Aging Reports

(C) Periodic Inventory Reports

(D) Physical Inventory Counts

Answers

1.(C),	2.(C),	3.(D),	4.(B),
5.(B),	6.(C),	7.(B),	8.(B).

DEBT MANAGEMENT: EMPOWERING SMES TO ACHIEVE FINANCIAL STABILITY

Debt management is a crucial aspect of running a Small and Medium Enterprise (SME). Managing debt effectively ensures that a business can sustain operations, invest in growth, and avoid financial pitfalls. This chapter will provide practical strategies for managing debt, along with real-life examples to illustrate these concepts.

13.1 Understanding Debt

Debt refers to borrowed money that must be repaid, usually with interest. SMEs often use debt to finance operations, purchase equipment, or expand their businesses. While debt can be a useful tool, mismanagement can lead to financial difficulties.

13.2 Types of Debt

1. **Short-term Debt**: Loans that need to be repaid within a year, such as credit lines or short-term bank loans.

2. **Long-term Debt**: Loans with a repayment period longer than a year, including term loans and mortgages.

3. **Trade Credit**: When suppliers allow businesses to pay for goods and services at a later date.

13.3 Key Principles of Debt Management

1. **Assessing the Need for Debt**

   Before taking on debt, it is essential to assess whether it is necessary. Ask questions like:

   o Do we need this debt for growth or to cover operational expenses?

   o Can we generate enough revenue to cover the debt repayments?

   Example:

   Sharma Furniture, a small business making custom furniture, needed a loan to purchase a new woodworking machine. They assessed their current orders and potential increase in production capacity with the new machine. Their calculations showed that the machine would increase revenue enough to cover the loan payments, making it a wise decision.

2. **Choosing the Right Type of Debt**

   Selecting the appropriate type of debt is crucial. Short-term debt is suitable for immediate needs like inventory purchases, while long-term debt is better for significant investments like new equipment.

   Example:

   Patel Café needed to renovate its premises to attract more customers. Instead of using a short-term loan with high-interest rates, they opted for a long-term loan with lower monthly payments, which fit better with their steady but moderate cash flow.

3. Understanding Interest Rates and Terms

Compare different loan offers and understand the interest rates, fees, and repayment terms. A lower interest rate can save a significant amount of money over the life of the loan.

Example:

Raju's Bakery needed a ₹40,00,000 loan. They received offers from two banks: Bank A offered a 7% interest rate, and Bank B offered a 9% interest rate. Over a five-year period, choosing Bank A saved Raju's Bakery nearly ₹3,00,000 in interest payments.

4. Maintaining a Healthy Cash Flow

Effective debt management requires a healthy cash flow to ensure timely repayments. Monitor your cash flow closely, and create a budget to manage your expenses and income.

Example:

Lisa's Boutique struggled with cash flow issues due to seasonal fluctuations in sales. By creating a detailed budget and setting aside funds during high-sales periods, they ensured they could make loan payments during slower months.

5. Prioritizing Debt Repayment

If an SME has multiple debts, it is vital to prioritize repayments. Focus on paying off high-interest debt first to reduce overall interest expenses.

Example:

Tech Solutions had three loans: a high-interest credit card debt, a medium-interest personal loan, and a low-interest business loan. They prioritized repaying the credit card debt first, followed by the personal loan, and then the business loan, saving them money on interest in the long run.

13.4 Strategies for Effective Debt Management

1. **Consolidating Debt**
   Debt consolidation involves combining multiple debts into a single loan with a lower interest rate. This simplifies repayments and can reduce interest costs.

   Example:

   Digital Innovations had multiple small loans with varying interest rates. They consolidated these into a single loan with a lower interest rate, reducing their monthly payments and simplifying their financial management.

2. **Renegotiating Terms**
   If cash flow becomes tight, renegotiate the terms of your loans with lenders. They may extend the repayment period or lower interest rates to help you manage better.

   Example:

   Green Landscaping faced a downturn and struggled to meet its loan payments. They approached their bank and negotiated an extended repayment period, which lowered their monthly payments and helped them stay afloat.

3. **Utilizing Financial Advisors**
   Financial advisors can provide valuable insights and strategies for managing debt effectively. They can help SMEs understand complex financial products and create a sustainable debt repayment plan.

   Example:

   Healthy Living, a small health store, hired a financial advisor when their debts became overwhelming. The advisor helped them consolidate debts, create a realistic budget, and negotiate better terms with their lenders.

13.5 Real-Life Case Study

Priya's Flower Shop

- **Background**: Priya's Flower Shop, an SME specializing in floral arrangements, experienced a surge in demand. To keep up, Priya took a ₹16,00,000 loan to buy new equipment and hire staff.
- **Challenges**: Six months later, Priya struggled with cash flow due to seasonal dips in sales and high-interest loan payments.

Solution:

1. **Assessment**: Priya assessed her debt and cash flow, identifying that the high-interest loan was the main burden.
2. **Debt Consolidation**: She consolidated her high-interest loan with a lower-interest business loan, reducing her monthly payments.
3. **Budgeting**: Priya created a detailed budget to manage her seasonal cash flow better, setting aside funds during peak seasons to cover lean periods.
4. **Negotiation**: She negotiated with her suppliers for extended payment terms, improving her short-term cash flow.
5. **Outcome**: Within a year, Priya's Flower Shop stabilized its cash flow, met all debt obligations, and continued to grow.

Conclusion

Effective debt management is essential for the sustainability and growth of SMEs. By assessing the need for debt, choosing the right type, understanding terms, maintaining cash flow, and prioritizing repayment, businesses can manage their debt responsibly. Utilizing strategies like debt consolidation, renegotiating terms, and seeking financial advice can further enhance debt management. Through careful planning and proactive management, SMEs can turn debt into a tool for growth rather than a burden.

Remember, managing debt effectively is about balancing risk and opportunity, ensuring that your business remains healthy and competitive in the long run

* * *

Chapter Challenge: Test Your Understanding with MCQs

1. **Why is it important to assess the need for debt before taking it on?**

   (A) To ensure there is enough collateral

   (B) To understand if the debt is necessary for growth or operations

   (C) To determine the credit score

   (D) To calculate the exact amount of interest

2. **What is a key advantage of choosing a long-term loan over a short-term loan?**

   (A) Higher interest rates

   (B) Lower monthly payments

   (C) Increased flexibility in spending

   (D) Immediate cash availability

3. **Which principle of debt management involves comparing different loan offers to save money on interest payments?**

   (A) Assessing the need for debt

   (B) Choosing the right type of debt

   (C) Understanding interest rates and terms

   (D) Prioritizing debt repayment

4. **What should a business do if it has multiple debts and wants to reduce overall interest expenses?**

    (A) Consolidate all debts

    (B) Renegotiate all terms at once

    (C) Prioritize repaying high-interest debt first

    (D) Focus on the smallest debt amount first

5. **Which strategy involves combining multiple debts into a single loan to simplify repayments and reduce interest costs?**

    (A) Renegotiating terms

    (B) Debt consolidation

    (C) Hiring a financial advisor

    (D) Creating a budget

Answers

1.(B),   2.(B),   3.(C),   4.(C),   5.(B)

CHAPTER 14

BALANCING THE BOOKS: RECONCILIATION IS THE KEY

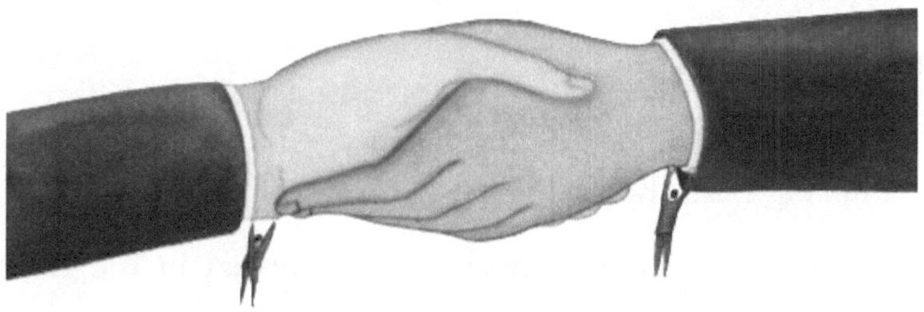

Reconciliation is a critical process in accounting that ensures the accuracy and integrity of financial records. For small and medium-sized enterprises (SMEs), maintaining accurate financial records is essential for effective management, compliance, and decision-making. Here are the key reasons why reconciliation is important:

1. **Accuracy of Financial Statements:** Reconciliation helps in identifying and correcting discrepancies between different sets of financial records. This ensures that the financial statements accurately reflect the true financial position of the business.

2. **Fraud Detection and Prevention:** Regular reconciliation can help detect unauthorized transactions, errors, or fraudulent activities. Early detection can prevent significant financial losses.

3. **Cash Flow Management:** By reconciling bank statements and cash accounts, SMEs can ensure they have accurate information about their cash position, aiding in better cash flow management and planning.

4. **Compliance with Regulations:** Accurate records are necessary for complying with tax laws and other regulatory requirements. Reconciliation ensures that the records used for compliance purposes are correct and complete.

5. **Better Decision-Making:** Reliable financial information is crucial for making informed business decisions. Reconciliation ensures that managers have accurate data to base their decisions on.

14.1   Types of Reconciliations Required

1. **Bank Reconciliation:**

   o **Purpose:** To compare the business's bank statement with its internal Bank Book.

   o **Process:** Match the transactions recorded in the company's cash book with those on the bank statement. Identify and investigate any discrepancies, such as unrecorded transactions, bank fees, or errors.

2. **GST Reconciliation:**

   o **Purpose:** To ensure that the Goods and Services Tax (GST) records match between the company's books and the GST returns filed.

   o **Process:** Compare the sales and purchase data recorded in the accounting system with the GST returns submitted to the tax authorities. Resolve any differences to ensure accurate tax reporting and compliance.

3. **Party Balance Reconciliation (Accounts Receivable and Accounts Payable):**

   o **Purpose:** To ensure that the balances owed by customers (accounts receivable) and the balances owed to suppliers (accounts payable) are accurate.

   o **Process:** For accounts receivable, reconcile customer statements with the ledger balances. For accounts payable, reconcile supplier statements with the payable ledger. Address any inconsistencies by investigating missing or duplicate entries, incorrect amounts, or unapplied credits.

4. **Inventory Reconciliation:**

   o **Purpose:** To verify that the physical inventory matches the recorded inventory levels.

   o **Process:** Conduct physical counts of inventory and compare the counts to the inventory records in the accounting system. Investigate and resolve discrepancies, such as shrinkage, theft, or data entry errors.

5. **Intercompany Reconciliation:**

   o **Purpose:** For businesses with multiple entities, to ensure that intercompany transactions and balances are accurately recorded and eliminated in the consolidated financial statements.

   o **Process:** Match the transactions recorded in one entity's books with the corresponding entries in the other entity's books. Reconcile any differences to ensure the integrity of consolidated financial data.

6. **Loan and Debt Reconciliation:**

   o **Purpose:** To ensure that loan balances and debt-related transactions are accurately recorded.

   o **Process:** Reconcile the loan statements from lenders with the company's records. Verify principal repayments, interest payments, and any additional charges or fees.

7. **Payroll Reconciliation:**

   o **Purpose:** To confirm that payroll records match the actual payments made to employees and related tax filings.

   o **Process:** Compare payroll registers and records with bank statements, tax filings, and other payroll-related documents. Ensure that all wages, deductions, and tax payments are accurately recorded.

Conclusion

Reconciliation is an ongoing process that requires diligence and attention to detail. For SMEs, regular reconciliation is vital to maintain the accuracy and integrity of financial records, detect and prevent fraud, ensure compliance with regulations, and provide a solid foundation for sound financial management and decision-making. Each type of reconciliation addresses different aspects of the business's financial operations, collectively contributing to a comprehensive and reliable accounting system. Here are some sample reconciliation formats that readers may use to reconcile the Ledgers with the records of third party

14.2   Format -1: Bank Reconciliation

ABC & Co.
BANK RECONCILIATION STATEMENT
FINANCIAL YEAR 20.. - ...
.... BANK - A/C .... MARCH ....

Particulars		Amount
Balance as per Cash book/Bank Book (Dr)		-
ADD: Cheques issued but not presented for payment		
Date Cheque no. Party Name Clearing Date	Amount	-
LESS: Cheque Deposited by us but not cleared by Bank		
Date Cheque no. Party Name Clearing Date	Amount	-
ADD: Credited by Bank but not in our record		
Date Cheque no. Party Name Recording Date	Amount	-
LESS: Debited by Bank but not in our record		
Date Cheque no. Party Name Recording Date	Amount	-
Balance as per Bank statement (Cr)		-

14.3 Format -2.1: Gst Turnover Reconciliation

GST RECO CHART- For Turnover (3B & Books)	
Particulars	**Amount**
GST Turnover As Per 3B—- A	
GST Turnover As Per Books——B	
Difference (A-B)	

Reconciliation of GST Turnover Difference (3B & Books)		
Particulars	**Amount**	**Reason for Difference**
GST Turnover as per 3B		
<u>Add: Turonver Shown in the Books & Not in 3B Return</u> Month- Month- 2 Month- ...		
<u>Less: Turonver Shown in the 3B Return & Not in Books</u> Month- 1 Month- 2 Month- ...		
GST Turnover as per Books		

GST RECO CHART- For Turnover (1 & 3B)	
Particulars	**Amount**
GST Turnover As Per GSTR 3B—- A	
GST Turnover As Per GSTR 1——B	
Difference (A-B)	

Reconciliation of GST Turnover Difference (1 & 3B)		
Particulars	**Amount**	**Reason for Difference**
GST Turnover as per 3B		
<u>Add: Turnover Shown in the GSTR 1 & Not in 3B Return</u>		
Month-1		
Month- …		
<u>Less: Turnover Shown in the 3B Return & Not in GSTR 1</u>		
Month- 1		
Month- …		
GST TURNOVER As per GSTR 1		

14.4   Format -2.2: Gst Itc Reconciliation

GST RECO CHART- For ITC GST RECO CHART			
PARTICULARS	**As Per 3B**	**As Per Books**	**Difference**
Opening Balance of ITC (Put Negative Sign if Payable)			
Add: ITC Availed During the period (Net of Reversal)			
Add: Challan Paid During the Year (Excluding for Late Fees and Intt)			
Total- A			
Less: Outward Liability during the Year- B			
Balance of ITC (Put Negative Sign if Payable)			

PERIOD: APRIL 2024 TO March 2025	
ITC Availed & Utilized as per Books & GSTR 3B- Difference Statement	**Amount**
ITC Availed & Utilized as per Books during April 2024 to March 2025	
ITC Availed & Utilized as per GSTR-3B during April 2024 to March 2025	
Difference in ITC Availed & Utilized i.e. Excess GST Utilized in GSTR 3B	

Reconciliation Statement	Amount
ITC Availed & Utilized as per Books during April 2024 to March 2025	
Add: Eligible ITC **Not taken** in Books but the same is **taken** in 2B/3B (As Per Annexure-A)	
Less: Eligible ITC taken in Books but the same **not taken** in 2B/3B (As Per Annexure-B)	
Less: Ineligible ITC **taken** in Books but the same **not taken** in 2B/3B (As Per Annexure-C)	
Add: Ineligible ITC Not **taken** in Books but the same is **taken** in 2B/3B (As Per Annexure-D)	
Add: ITC **Reversed** in Books due to Credit Note Received but Input Tax credit already taken in 3B (As Per Annexure-E)	
Less: ITC **not Reversed** in Books But Credit Note Received & Input Tax credit already reversed in 3B (As Per Annexure-F)	
ITC Availed & Utilized as per GSTR-3B during April 2024 to March 2025	

Eligible ITC Not taken in Books but the same is taken in 2B/3B (Annexure A)								
Bill Date	**Party Name**	**GST No.**	**Bill No.**	**Gross Amt**	**SGST**	**CGST**	**IGST**	**Total GST**

ITC taken in Books but the same not taken in 2B/3B (Annexure B)								
Bill Date	**Party**	**GST No.**	**Bill No.**	**Gross Amt**	**SGST**	**CGST**	**IGST**	**Total GST**

Ineligible ITC taken in Books but the same not taken in 2B/3B (Annexure C)								
Bill Date	Party Name	GST No.	Bill No.	Gross Amt	SGST	CGST	IGST	Total GST

Ineligible ITC Not taken in Books but the same is taken in 2B/3B (Annexure D)								
Bill Date	Party Name	GST No.	Bill No.	Gross Amt	SGST	CGST	IGST	Total GST

ITC Reversed in Books due to Credit Note Received but Input Tax credit already taken in 3B (Annexure E)											
Party Name	GST No.	Bill no.	Month	CN No.	CN Date	Type	Gross	SGST	CGST	IGST	Total GST

ITC not Reversed in Books But Credit Note Received & Input Tax credit already reversed in 3B (Annexure F)											
Party Name	GST No.	Bill no.	Month	CN No.	CN Date	Type	Gross	SGST	CGST	IGST	Total GST

14.5   Format -3.1: Debtor Reconciliation

ABC & Co.

FINANCIAL YEAR 20.. - ...

PARTY NAME .... (Debtors/ Customer)

Particulars		Amount
Party Balances in Our Books (Dr)		
ADD: Credit Note issued by us but not recorded by the Customer Date CN No.	Amount	-
LESS: Debit Note issued by us but not recorded by the Customer Date DN No.	Amount	-
LESS: Debit note issued by the Customer but not recorded by us Date DN No.	Amount	-
LESS: Payment Made by the Customer but not recorded in our Books Date Payment Details	Amount	-
ADD: Payment of some other Party posted in Ledger Account Date Payment Details	Amount	-
Balance as per Party statement (Cr)		-

14.6   Format -3.2: Creditor Reconciliation

ABC & Co.

FINANCIAL YEAR 20.. - ...

PARTY NAME .... (Creditor/Suuplier)

Particulars		Amount
Party Balances in Our Books (Cr)		
ADD: Debit Note issued by us but not recorded by the Supplier		
Date CN No.	Amount	-
LESS: Credit note issued by the Supplier but not recorded by us		
Date DN No.	Amount	-
ADD: Payment Made to the Supplier but not recorded in his Books		
Date Payment Details	Amount	-
ADD: Payment of some other Party posted in Ledger Account		
Date Payment Details	Amount	-
Balance as per Party statement (Dr)		-

14.7 Format -4: Inventory Reconciliation

Sr No.	Material Description	Serial no.	System Qty	Physical Qty	Variance	Reason for Variance

Reason for Variance May Include:

1. Sent for Job Work

2. Lost (Debit Note issued)

3. Lost (Debit Note Not Issued)

4. Sample held by field executive

5. Defective (held in stock)

6. Any Other

* * *

Chapter Challenge: Test Your Understanding with MCQs

1. Why is reconciliation important for SMEs?

(A) It helps in identifying new business opportunities.

(B) It ensures the accuracy and integrity of financial records.

(C) It primarily focuses on customer satisfaction.

(D) It reduces the need for external audits.

2. **What is the main purpose of bank reconciliation?**

    (A) To compare the company's bank book with the bank statement.

    (B) To prepare for annual financial audits.

    (C) To update customer contact information.

    (D) To analyze market trends.

3. **Which type of reconciliation ensures the accuracy of balances owed by customers and to suppliers?**

    (A) Bank Reconciliation

    (B) GST Reconciliation

    (C) Party Balance Reconciliation

    (D) Inventory Reconciliation

4. **What process is involved in inventory reconciliation?**

    (A) Comparing physical counts of inventory to the inventory records in the accounting system.

    (B) Matching payroll registers with bank statements.

    (C) Reconciling loan statements with company records.

    (D) Ensuring GST records match the GST returns filed.

5. **What is a key benefit of regular reconciliation for SMEs?**

    (A) It simplifies the marketing strategies.

    (B) It reduces employee turnover.

    (C) It aids in better cash flow management and planning.

    (D) It enhances customer loyalty programs.

Answers

1.(B),   2.(A),   3.(C),   4.(A),   5.(C)

CHAPTER 15

IMPLEMENTATION GUIDE FOR ESTABLISHING A ROBUST ACCOUNTING SYSTEM

1. Hiring Qualified Staff

- ○ **Identify Needs:** As you are now self-sufficient to assess your accounts volume and complexity of your accounting tasks, you need to assess whether you require a mid-level accountant or expert level accountant or combination of both.

- ○ **Experience:** Prioritize candidates with experience in your industry or with SMEs, as they will better understand your specific challenges.

- ○ **Interview Process:** Use a structured interview process to evaluate technical skills, ask about the fundamentals of accounting, software proficiency, and cultural fit.

2. Preparing Standard Operating Procedures (SOPs)

- **Documentation:** Create detailed SOPs for all accounting processes, including invoicing, expense tracking, payroll, and financial reporting.

- **Consistency:** Ensure that SOPs promote consistency in how transactions are recorded and processed.

- **Training:** Regularly train staff on SOPs to ensure adherence and update them as needed to reflect changes in regulations or business processes.

Bonus: A sample SOP is mentioned in **Appendix- 1.**

3. Setting Up a Chart of Accounts

- **Customization:** Design a chart of accounts tailored to your business's specific needs, ensuring it captures all relevant categories of income, expenses, assets, liabilities, and equity.

- **Standardization:** Follow standard accounting practices to ensure your chart of accounts is easy to understand and can be used for financial analysis and reporting.

- **Review:** Periodically review and update the chart of accounts to reflect any changes in the business structure or operations.

Bonus: A sample SOP is mentioned in **Appendix- 2**

4. Printing Vouchers and Documentation

- **Templates:** Develop standard templates for invoices, receipts, payment vouchers, and expense reports. Formats of the same are already discussed earlier

- **Compliance:** Ensure that these documents meet legal and regulatory requirements, including necessary information such as tax identification numbers and business addresses.

- **Automation:** Use accounting software to automate the generation and tracking of these documents to reduce errors and save time.

5. Implementing Accounting Software

- **Selection:** Choose accounting software that fits the size and complexity of your business. Consider features like ease of use, integration with other systems, scalability, and customer support. Preferred Accounting Software are Tally, Busy etc.

- **Training:** Invest in training for your staff to ensure they can effectively use the software.

- **Data Migration:** Carefully plan and execute the migration of your existing financial data to the new system, ensuring data accuracy and completeness.

- **Regular Updates:** Keep your software updated to benefit from the latest features and security patches.

6. Keeping a Compliance Calendar

- **Deadlines:** Maintain a calendar of key compliance deadlines, including tax filings, financial reporting, payroll submissions, and regulatory filings.

- **Reminders:** Set up automated reminders to ensure deadlines are not missed.

- **Review:** Regularly review compliance requirements to stay updated with any changes in laws and regulations affecting your business.

Bonus: A sample Compliance Calendar is mentioned in **Appendix- 3**

7. Regular Financial Reviews

- **Monthly Closings:** Conduct monthly closing procedures to ensure all financial transactions are recorded and reconciled.

- **Reporting:** Generate and review financial statements regularly (e.g., income statement, balance sheet, cash flow statement) to monitor the financial health of your business.

- **Analysis:** Use financial ratios and metrics to analyze performance and make informed business decisions.

8. **Internal Controls**

- **Segregation of Duties:** Implement controls to segregate accounting duties among different staff members to prevent fraud and errors.

- **Authorization:** Establish authorization protocols for financial transactions, ensuring that all expenditures are approved by the appropriate personnel.

- **Audits:** Conduct periodic internal audits to review and strengthen your accounting processes and controls.

9. **Establishing a Budgeting Process**

- **Forecasting:** Develop financial forecasts to guide your budgeting process, considering historical data and future business goals.

- **Allocation:** Allocate resources based on strategic priorities and operational needs.

- **Monitoring:** Regularly compare actual performance against the budget to identify variances and make necessary adjustments.

10. **Leveraging Financial Advice**

- **Consultation:** Engage with financial advisors or consultants to gain expert insights on complex financial matters.

- **Networking:** Participate in industry forums and networking events to stay informed about best practices and emerging trends in accounting and finance.

- **Continuous Learning:** Encourage continuous learning and professional development for your accounting staff to keep up with the latest industry standards and technologies.

15.1 Appendix 1 – Sample Accounts SOP

Sr. No.	Activity	By Whom	By When
1.	Budgeting	Mgmt.	01st April
2.	Compilation of All Expense Bills	Mgmt./ Acct.	Daily
3.	Preparation of Payment & Journal Vouchers	Acct.	Daily
4.	Entry in Accounting Software of Expense Vouchers	Acct.	Daily
5.	Income: Preparation & Issuance of Bills (Invoices). • Directly in Accounting Software or • Prepare Bills in an excel format	Acct.	Daily
6.	Updation of All Bills (GST/ Non GST Invoice) in Accounting Software (if Prepared in excel)	Acct.	Immediately after Bill Issuance
7.	Downloading/ Collection of All Bank Statement including all Loans & UPI Statement	Acct.	Daily/ As Required (Mandatory on 1st Day of next Month)
8.	Following entries must be done in Accounting Software: 1. All Bills/ Invoices 2. All Expense Vouchers 3. All Bank Statements	Acct.	By 6th of Next Month
9.	Filing of GSTR- 1 (If GST Registered)	CA/ Acct.	By 8th of Next month
10.	Verification of GSTR- 2B & Purchase Bills as per List	Mgmt./Acct.	By 14th of next Month/ As Per Payment Terms
11.	Filing of GSTR-3B (If GST Registered)	CA/ Acct.	By 15th of Next month
12.	Statutory Liabilities: Following Payments must be made as per the Accounts: A. TDS Payable B. GST Payable C. Advance Tax D. PF & ESI E. Any Other Taxes	Acct.	 By 7th of Next Month By 20th of Next Month By 15th of Next Month (Or as per ITD Schedule) By 15th of Next Month As Applicable

Sr. No.	Activity	By Whom	By When
13.	<u>Prepare Reconciliation Statements</u> -Bank Reconciliation -GST Reconciliation -Party Reconciliation -Inventory Control -TDS reconciliation	Mgmt.	By 20th of Next month/ As required
14.	Updation of all Left over entries/ correction entries in Accounting Software	Acct.	By 20th of Next Month
15.	Debtors Follow up	Mgmt./Acct	By 25th of next Month/ As Per Payment Terms
16.	Filing of TDS Return	CA/ Acct.	By 15th after Quarter End
17.	Collection & Matching of Form 26AS/ 16A/ GSTR- 7A with TDS Deducted by party on our invoice	Mgmt./Acct.	GSTR-7A (Monthly) (In Case of Govt Pay.) Others: Within 45 Days after the end of every Quarter
18.	Downloading & Mailing of TDS Certificates	CA/Acct.	By 30th of the end of each Quarter
19.	Review of Balance Sheet (Ledger scrutiny)	Mgmt.	By 30th after the end of every Quarter
20.	Ratio Analysis	Mgmt.	By 30th after the end of every Quarter
21.	Actual vs. Budget Analysis	Mgmt.	By 30th after the end of every Quarter
22.	Internal Audit/ Risk Assessment	Mgmt.	By 30th after the end of every Quarter
22.	Company/LLP ROC Compliances	CA/CS	As required
23.	Statutory Audit & IT Return Filing	CA	By 30th June/30th Sep. at the end of year or asap

Note: This is a sample List for reference purpose only. Users are advised to create their own Account Process SOP by adding/ deleting certain Items

15.2   Appendix 2 – Sample Chart of Accounts

Group Name	Ledger Name
Purchase Accounts	**All types of Purchase Accounts like**
	Purchase Within State 18%
	Purchase Interstate 18%
	Purchase Within State 0%
	Purchase Interstate 0%
	Purchase (Composition)
	Purchase Exempt (Unregistered Dealer)
	Purchase Within State (Exempt Registered)
	Purchase Taxable (Unregistered Dealer)
	Purchase Nil Rated (Unregistered Dealer)
	Purchase Reverse Charge
	Purchase Import Taxable 18%
	Purchase Import Exempt
	Purchase Import Nil Rated
	Purchase (Own Branch)
	Purchase Return (Cr.)

Group Name	Ledger Name
Sales Account	**All types of Sales Accounts like**
	Sales Within State 18% (Registered) (B2B)
	Sales Interstate 18% (B2B)
	Sales Within Nil Rated (B2B)
	Sales Interstate Nil Rated (B2B)
	Sales Export With Bond
	Sales Export Taxable
	Export (0%)
	Sales Within State (Exempt Registered)
	Sale To Consumer (B2C)(Taxable 12%)
	Sale To Consumer (B2C) (0%)
	Sale To Consumer (B2C)(Exempt)
	Sales (Own Branch)
	Sale Return (Dr.)
Duties and Taxes	**All types of Taxes like**
	INPUT CGST SGST IGST CESS
	OUTPUT GST SGST IGST CESS
	Excise Duty Payable etc
	Service Tax Payable
	TDS Payables
	Input Vat Accounts
	Output Vat Accounts
	Cenvat Accounts
	Sale tax
	Income Tax
	VAT Payable

Group Name	Ledger Name
Direct Expenses OR Expenses (Direct)	**All expenses which appear in Trading Account (except purchases) like**
	Labor
	Power
	Electricity Expense (Factory)
	Loading Unloading Expense
	Warehousing Expenses
	Custom Clearing Charges
	Carriage
	Freight & Cartage
	Import duty
	Wages
	Coal & Fuel
	Coal, Gas & Water of Factory
	Consumed Material
	Export Duty
	Wages on Production
	Delivery Charges Etc.
Indirect Expenses OR Expense (Indirect)	**All Indirect Expenses like**
	Rounded Off
	Salary
	Advertisement Expense
	Maintenance Expense
	Rent Expense
	Director Remuneration Expense
	Bad Debts
	Printing Expense
	Stationary Expense
	Foreign Exchange fluctuation

Group Name	Ledger Name
Indirect Expenses OR Expense (Indirect)	Audit Fees
	Professional Charges
	Legal Expenses/Charges
	Interest Expense
	Penalty
	Royalty
	Bank charges
	Commission allowed
	Discount allowed
	Donation & charity
	Stock Insurance premium
	Interest on loan
	Legal charge
	Postage & courier
	Repair charge
	Taxi fare
	Telephone charge
	Travelling expenses
	Outstanding expenses
	Accrued expenses
	Depreciation
	Coffee Expenses
	Manager's Commission
	Fuel Expenses A/c
	Preliminary Expenses A/c
	Professional Fees Etc.

Group Name	Ledger Name
Indirect Income OR Income (Indirect)	**All Indirect Income like**
	Discount Received
	Interest on Investment
Bank Account	**All Bank Current Account**
	All Bank FD Account
Deposit Account	**All types of deposits like**
	Security Deposit
	Electricity Deposit
	Rent Deposit
Capital A/c	**All types of Capital Account like**
	Share Capital
	Partner Capital Account
	Partner Current Account
	Proprietor Account
	Drawings
	Life insurance
	Equity Capital A/c
	Partners' Capital A/c

Group Name	Ledger Name
Current Assets	Prepaid Maintenance Expense
	Prepaid Expense
	Prepaid Rent
	Prepaid Insurance Charges
	Interest Receivables
	Bill receivable
	Accrued income
Current Liabilities	Bill drawn
	Bill Payable
Sundry Creditor	Any Party from Whom Goods Purchased
	Party from Whom any Bill of Expense Received
Loans and Advances (Assets)	**Any Party to whom we gave loan**
	like Loan Given to Friends Relatives/Related Companies
	Any Party to whom we gave Advance
	like Advance to Supplier
Loans (Liabilities)	**Any Party from whom we take loan.**
	We can also put group Secured loan or Unsecured loan
	Debenture A/c
	Loans From Bank
	Loans From Outside Party
	Loans From Aravind(Friend)

Group Name	Ledger Name
	All Fixed Assets on which Depreciation charged like
	Furniture
	Machine
	Plant and Machinery
	Mobile
	Computers
	Furniture and Fittings
Fixed Assets	Car
	Scooter
	Laptops
	Office lighting
	Land & Building
	Good will
	Factory lighting
	Air Conditioner
Bank OCC	**Cash Credit Limit (CC)**
	taken from bank
Bank OD	**Overdraft Limit (OD)**
	taken from bank
Branch/ Divisions	**Any Branch whose Separate Accounting Done**
	(If branch account maintained by head office only, then this account not required)
	Delhi Branch
	Branch in division

Group Name	Ledger Name
Cash in Hand	**Imprest Account**
	(Cash kept with Employee)
	Petty Cash
Investments	**All types of Investments like**
	Investment in Shares
	Investment in Bonds
	Investment in Property/Plot etc.
	Long term investment
	Short Term Investment
Stock-in-hand	Stock
	Closing Stock
	Consignment Stock
	Opening Stock
Misc. Expense (ASSET)	**Preliminary Expenses**
	NOT yet written off
Suspense A/c	**Suspense Account**
	Any payment or receipt from party whose name not known
	Suspense
Secured Loan	**Loans for whom Security Given**
	like loan from bank/ Financial Institution
Unsecured Loan	**Loans taken for whom no Security given**
	Like Short term loan from directors
	or loan from friends /relatives

Group Name	Ledger Name
Reserve & Surplus	**Any type of reserve like**
	General Reserve
	Capital Reserve
	Capital Reserve A/c
	Investment Allowance Reserve A/c
	Share Premium A/c
	Reverse and Surplus
Provisions	**All Provisions except Provisions for bad debts**
	Provision for Tax
	Provision for Expense
	Provision for Sinking Fund
	All types of Payables like Salary Payable, Audit fees Payable,
Sundry Debtors	**Any Party to Whom Sales Made**
	Provision for Bad Debts
Retained Earring	General Reserve
	Share Premium
	Any other Reserve
Direct Incomes OR Income (Direct)	**Any Income from main service like**
	Freight Charges Income
	Delivery Charges Income
	Transportation Charges Income
	Professional Charges Income
	Consultancy Charges Income
	Maintenance Service Income

15.3 Appendix 3 – Compliance Calendar

April- 2024			May- 2024		
SR NO.	**INCOME TAX COMPLIANCES**	**DUE DATE**	**SR NO.**	**INCOME TAX COMPLIANCES**	**DUE DATE**
1	TCS Payment for March 24	7th April 2024	1	TDS/TCS Payment for April 24	7th May 2024
2	TDS Payment for March 24	30th April 2024	2	TCS Return for 4th Qtr	15th May 2024
			3	Issuance of TCS Cert. (March Qtr)	30th May 2024
			4	TDS Return for March 24	31th May 2024
			5	Form 61-A (SFT)	31th May 2024
			6	Form 10BD (Donation)	31th May 2024

June- 2024			July- 2024		
SR NO.	**INCOME TAX COMPLIANCES**	**DUE DATE**	**SR NO.**	**INCOME TAX COMPLIANCES**	**DUE DATE**
1	TDS/TCS Payment for May 24	7th June 2024	1	TDS/TCS Payment for June 24	7th July 2024
2	Advance Tax Payment (1st Qtr)	15th June 2024	2	TCS Return for 1st Qtr	15th July 2024
3	Issuance of TDS Cert. (March Qtr)	15th June 2024	3	Issuance of TCS Cert. (June Qtr)	30th July 2024
			4	TDS Return for 1st Qtr	31st July 2024
			5	Filing of ITR (Non Audit)	31st July 2024

June- 2024			July- 2024		
SR NO.	**GST COMPLIANCES**	**DUE DATE**	**SR NO.**	**GST COMPLIANCES**	**DUE DATE**
1	GSTR-7 (Monthly) for May- TDS	10th June 2024	1	GSTR-7 (Monthly) for June- TDS	10th July 2024
2	GSTR-1 (Monthly) for May	11th June 2024	2	GSTR-1 (Monthly) for June	11th July 2024
3	GSTR-3B (Monthly) for May	20th June 2024	3	GSTR-1 (QRMP) for June	13th July 2024
			4	CMP-08 (Composition)- June Qtr	18th July 2024
			5	GSTR-3B (Monthly) for June	20th July 2024

SR NO.	**ROC COMPLIANCES**	**DUE DATE**	**SR NO.**	**ROC COMPLIANCES**	**DUE DATE**
1	DPT-3	30th June 2024	1	NIL	

August- 2024			September- 2024		
SR NO.	**INCOME TAX COMPLIANCES**	**DUE DATE**	**SR NO.**	**INCOME TAX COMPLIANCES**	**DUE DATE**
1	TDS/TCS Payment for July 24	7th August 2024	1	TDS/TCS Payment for August 24	7th Sep 2024
2	Issuance of TDS Cert. (June Qtr)	15th August 2024	2	Advance Tax Payment (2nd Qtr)	15th Sep 2024
			3	Tax Audit	30th Sep 2024
			4	Company Audit	30th Sep 2024
			5	Society Audit	30th Sep 2024
			6	All Other Audits	30th Sep 2024

	August- 2024			September- 2024	
SR NO.	GST COMPLIANCES	DUE DATE	SR NO.	GST COMPLIANCES	DUE DATE
1	GSTR-7 (Monthly) for July- TDS	10th Aug 2024	1	GSTR-7 (Monthly) for Aug- TDS	10th Sep 2024
2	GSTR-1 (Monthly) for July	11th Aug 2024	2	GSTR-1 (Monthly) for Aug	11th Sep 2024
3	GSTR-3B (Monthly) for July	20th Aug 2024	3	GSTR-3B (Monthly) for Aug	20th Sep 2024

SR NO.	ROC COMPLIANCES	DUE DATE	SR NO.	ROC COMPLIANCES	DUE DATE
	NIL		1	E-Kyc	30th Sep 2024

	October- 2024			November- 2024	
SR NO.	INCOME TAX COMPLIANCES	DUE DATE	SR NO.	INCOME TAX COMPLIANCES	DUE DATE
1	TDS/TCS Payment for Sep 24	7th Oct 2024	1	TDS/TCS Payment for October 24	7th Nov. 2024
2	TCS Return for 2nd Qtr	15th Oct 2024	2	Issuance of TDS Cert. (Sep Qtr)	15th Nov 2024
3	Issuance of TCS Cert. (Sep Qtr)	30th Oct 2024			
4	TDS Return for 2nd Qtr	31st Oct 2024			
5	Filing of ITR (Audit Cases)	31st Oct 2024			

October- 2024			November- 2024		
SR NO.	GST COMPLIANCES	DUE DATE	SR NO.	GST COMPLIANCES	DUE DATE
1	GSTR-7 (Monthly) for Sep- TDS	10th Oct 2024	1	GSTR-7 (Monthly) for Oct- TDS	10th Nov 2024
2	GSTR-1 (Monthly) for Sep	11th Oct 2024	2	GSTR-1 (Monthly) for Oct	11th Nov 2024
3	GSTR-1 (QRMP) for Sep	13th Oct 2024	3	GSTR-3B (Monthly) for Oct	20th Nov 2024
4	CMP-08 (Composition)- Sep Qtr	18th Oct 2024	4	ITC 2B Reco with Bills- Upto Sep	20th Nov 2024
5	GSTR-3B (Monthly) for Sep	20th Oct 2024			

SR NO.	ROC COMPLIANCES	DUE DATE	SR NO.	ROC COMPLIANCES	DUE DATE
1	ADT-1 (Auditor App.)	13th Oct 2024	1	MGT-7/7A (AR)	27th Nov 2024
2	AOC-4 (FS)	28th Oct 2024			
3	Form-8 LLP	30th Oct 2024			

December- 2024			January- 2025		
SR NO.	INCOME TAX COMPLIANCES	DUE DATE	SR NO.	INCOME TAX COMPLIANCES	DUE DATE
1	TDS/TCS Payment for Nov 24	7th Dec 2024	1	TDS/TCS Payment for Dec 24	7th Jan 2025
2	Advance Tax Payment (3rd Qtr)	15th Dec 2024	2	TCS Return for 3rd Qtr	15th Jan 2025
			3	Issuance of TCS Cert. (Dec Qtr)	31st Jan 2025
			4	TDS Return for 3rd Qtr	31st Jan 2025

December- 2024			January- 2025		
SR NO.	GST COMPLIANCES	DUE DATE	SR NO.	GST COMPLIANCES	DUE DATE
1	GSTR-7 (Monthly) for Nov- TDS	10th Dec 2024	1	GSTR-7 (Monthly) for Dec- TDS	10th Jan 2025
2	GSTR-1 (Monthly) for Nov	11th Dec 2024	2	GSTR-1 (Monthly) for Dec	11th Jan 2025
3	GSTR-3B (Monthly) for Nov	20th Dec 2024	3	GSTR-1 (QRMP) for Dec	13th Jan 2025
4	GSTR-9 (AR) (Regular)	30th Dec 2024	4	CMP-08 (Composition)- Dec Qtr	18th Jan 2025
5	GSTR-9A (AR) (Composition)	30th Dec 2024	5	GSTR-3B (Monthly) for Dec	20th Jan 2025

SR NO.	ROC COMPLIANCES	DUE DATE	SR NO.	ROC COMPLIANCES	DUE DATE
	NIL			NIL	

February- 2025			March- 2025		
SR NO.	INCOME TAX COMPLIANCES	DUE DATE	SR NO.	INCOME TAX COMPLIANCES	DUE DATE
1	TDS/TCS Payment for Jan 24	7th Feb 2025	1	TDS/TCS Payment for Feb 24	7th March 2025
2	Issuance of TDS Cert. (Dec Qtr)	15th Feb 2025	2	Advance Tax Payment (4th Qtr)	15th March 2025

February- 2025			March- 2025		
SR NO.	GST COMPLIANCES	DUE DATE	SR NO.	GST COMPLIANCES	DUE DATE
1	GSTR-7 (Monthly) for Feb- TDS	10th Feb 2025	1	GSTR-7 (Monthly) for Feb- TDS	10th Mar 2025
2	GSTR-1 (Monthly) for Jan	11th Feb 2025	2	GSTR-1 (Monthly) for Feb	11th Mar 2025
3	GSTR-3B (Monthly) for Jan	20th Feb 2025	3	GSTR-3B (Monthly) for Feb	20th Mar 2025
			4	LUT (Export Cases)	20th Mar 2025
SR NO.	ROC COMPLIANCES	DUE DATE	SR NO.	ROC COMPLIANCES	DUE DATE
	NIL			NIL	

Note: Please note that the Compliance Calendar provided above serves as a general guideline and is not exhaustive. Various other Acts and Rules necessitate compliance obligations, each with its own set of requirements and deadlines contingent upon their respective statutes and the nature of the industry. Readers are encouraged to supplement this calendar with additional compliance obligations as per their specific needs and regulatory environment.

* * *

Chapter Challenge: Test Your Understanding with MCQs

1. **When hiring accounting staff, what is a key factor to prioritize?**

   (A) Candidates with experience in large multinational corporations

   (B) Candidates with experience in your specific industry or SMEs

   (C) Candidates with a background in sales

   (D) Candidates who are recent graduates

2. **What is the primary purpose of creating Standard Operating Procedures (SOPs) for accounting processes?**

   (A) To reduce the number of employees needed

   (B) To ensure consistency and adherence to processes

   (C) To increase the speed of financial reporting

   (D) To impress stakeholders with detailed documentation

3. **How often should the Chart of Accounts be reviewed and updated?**

   (A) Never, once it's set up

   (B) Only when there is a major business change

   (C) Periodically to reflect changes in the business structure or operations

   (D) Every week

4. **Why is it important to use templates for vouchers and documentation?**

   (A) To ensure compliance with legal and regulatory requirements

   (B) To make the documents look more professional

   (C) To save paper

   (D) To increase the number of transactions processed

5. **When implementing accounting software, what should be a key consideration?**

    (A) Choosing the most expensive software available

    (B) Selecting software that fits the size and complexity of your business

    (C) Ensuring the software can only be used by the accounting department

    (D) Picking software with the most features regardless of necessity

6. **What is the benefit of maintaining a compliance calendar?**

    (A) To keep track of employee birthdays

    (B) To ensure key compliance deadlines are met

    (C) To plan for company events

    (D) To schedule routine maintenance of office equipment

7. **Which activity should be included in regular financial reviews?**

    (A) Monthly closing procedures and generating financial statements

    (B) Daily check-ins with every employee

    (C) Weekly team-building activities

    (D) Monthly social media updates

8. **What is a critical component of establishing internal controls in accounting?**

    (A) Centralizing all financial tasks with one person

    (B) Implementing segregation of duties among different staff members

    (C) Increasing the workload on the accounting team

    (D) Using manual ledgers for all transactions

Answers:

1.(B),   2.(B),   3.(C),   4.(B),   5.(B),
6.(B),   7.(A),   8.(B)

MASTERING ACCURACY: COMMON ACCOUNTING ERRORS AND THEIR SOLUTIONS

Common Accounting Errors

Accountants, like all professionals, can make errors in their work. Common errors made by accountants & their solutions are mentioned below:

Sr No.	Common Errors	Type of Errors	Solution
1.	**Data Entry Errors:**	**Transposition errors**: Numbers are reversed (e.g., entering 543 instead of 453). **Misplacing decimals**: Entering incorrect decimal placements can drastically change figures. **Duplicate entries**: Entering the same transaction multiple times.	Double-check entries with vouchers, and implement a review process where another person verifies the entries.
2.	**Calculation Mistakes:**	**Incorrect addition or subtraction**: Simple arithmetic mistakes in vouchers can lead to significant discrepancies. **Formula errors in spreadsheets**: Incorrect formulas or cell references can produce incorrect totals.	Use accounting software with built-in calculation checks and regularly audit formulas and totals in spreadsheets.

Sr No.	Common Errors	Type of Errors	Solution
3.	**Incorrect Classification:**	**Misclassifying expenses and income**: Placing an expense in the wrong category or misclassifying income can distort financial reports. **Mixing personal and business expenses**: Not separating personal expenses from business expenses can lead to inaccurate financial statements.	Maintain clear guidelines for classification, use standardized chart of accounts, and conduct regular reviews to ensure correct classification.
4.	**Failure to Reconcile Accounts:**	**Bank reconciliation errors**: Failing to reconcile bank statements with the company's records can lead to unnoticed discrepancies. **Ignoring minor discrepancies**: Small differences, if ignored consistently, can accumulate into larger issues.	Schedule regular reconciliations, and investigate all discrepancies, no matter how minor.
5.	**Missing Transactions:**	**Overlooking transactions**: Forgetting to record a transaction can lead to incomplete financial records. **Failure to track petty cash:** Not accurately recording petty cash expenses can result in imbalanced accounts.	Implement a system for immediate transaction recording, regularly review accounts, and establish a petty cash log.
6.	**Errors in Documentation:**	**Inadequate documentation**: Failing to keep proper documentation for transactions can lead to issues during audits. **Misfiling documents:** Incorrectly filed documents can make it difficult to retrieve information when needed.	Develop a standardized documentation process, use digital document management systems, and ensure all transactions have supporting documents.
7.	**Non-compliance with Accounting Standards:**	**Not following AS/ Ind AS**: Deviating from Accounting standards can lead to incorrect financial reporting. **Ignoring regulatory updates:** Failing to stay updated with changes in tax laws or accounting regulations can result in non-compliance.	Regularly train staff on current accounting standards, subscribe to updates from regulatory bodies, and conduct periodic compliance audits.

Sr No.	Common Errors	Type of Errors	Solution
8.	**Timing Issues:**	**Incorrectly recognizing revenue and expenses:** Recording revenue or expenses in the wrong accounting period can misrepresent financial performance. **Late financial statements:** Delays in preparing financial statements can affect decision-making.	Follow accrual accounting principles, set clear cut-off policies for end-of-period transactions, and perform periodic reviews of revenue and expense entries.
9.	**Misinterpretation of Data:**	**Incorrect analysis:** Misinterpreting financial data can lead to poor business decisions. **Ignoring trends:** Failing to recognize and act on financial trends can prevent timely interventions.	Use robust financial analysis tools, provide training on financial analysis, and have multiple individuals review and interpret key data.
10.	**Errors in Tax Filing:**	**Incorrect tax calculations:** Mistakes in calculating taxes owed can lead to penalties. **Missing tax deductions or credits:** Failing to claim eligible deductions or credits can result in higher tax liabilities.	Be in touch with a qualified professional, take guidance regularly & stay informed on tax law changes

* * *

Chapter Challenge: Test Your Understanding with MCQs

1. **Which of the following errors is an example of a data entry error?**

   (A) Incorrectly classifying expenses

   (B) Failure to reconcile accounts

   (C) Entering the number 543 instead of 453

   (D) Ignoring regulatory updates

2. **What is the recommended solution to prevent calculation mistakes in spreadsheets?**

   (A) Implement a system for immediate transaction recording

   (B) Use accounting software with built-in calculation checks

   (C) Maintain clear guidelines for classification

   (D) Develop a standardized documentation process

3. **How can incorrect classification of expenses and income be prevented?**

   (A) Schedule regular reconciliations

   (B) Use standardized chart of accounts and conduct regular reviews

   (C) Implement a petty cash log

   (D) Regularly train staff on current accounting standards

4. **What should be done to avoid errors in documentation?**

   (A) Schedule regular reconciliations

   (B) Use robust financial analysis tools

   (C) Develop a standardized documentation process and use digital document management systems

   (D) Follow accrual accounting principles

5. Which of the following can help ensure compliance with accounting standards?

(A) Implement a review process where another person verifies the entries

(B) Schedule regular reconciliations

(C) Regularly train staff on current accounting standards and subscribe to updates from regulatory bodies

(D) Use robust financial analysis tools

6. What is the best practice to prevent unnoticed discrepancies between bank statements and the company's records?

(A) Implement a system for immediate transaction recording

(B) Use accounting software with built-in calculation checks

(C) Develop a standardized documentation process

(D) Do regular reconciliation

Answers:

1. (C),   2. (B),   3. (B),   4. (C),   5. (C),   6. (D).

CHAPTER 17

YEAR END TIPS: 14 MUST TO DO THINGS BEFORE MARCH CLOSING

1. Check Payable Advance Tax

- Review the advance tax paid for the last year and compare it with the current year's tax liabilities.

- Evaluate profits up to the Last quarter, estimate current year turnover and additional income, and pay advance tax monthly or quarterly to reduce interest charges.

2. Make Investments to Save Tax/Create Wealth/Reduce Risks

- Invest in life insurance and medical insurance to save tax and secure your financial future.

- Consider investments in Public Provident Fund (PPF), National Pension System (NPS), and mutual funds (debt, equity, ELSS) for wealth creation and tax benefits.

3. Minimize Debtor & Creditor Balances

o Reconcile debtor, creditor, and party balances to ensure accuracy.

o Make and receive payments promptly and obtain and provide MSME certificates to improve financial ratios and avoid additions under Section 43B(h) for non-payment to small and medium enterprises.

4. Find Out Capital Gains

o Calculate capital gains tax on any property, capital assets, or liquidated investments like mutual funds and pay advance tax accordingly.

o Plan investments to save on capital gains tax, if applicable.

5. Purchase of Fixed Assets for Business

o Buy planned assets such as machinery, computers, printers, furniture, and electronics before the financial year-end to claim additional depreciation.

o Plan new loans within the current month as banks aim to meet their targets.

6. Manage Physical Inventory

o Conduct stock verification quarterly or at least at the financial year-end and reconcile with books of accounts.

o Clean up obsolete stock and bifurcate closing stock into categories like raw material, finished goods, WIP, and consumables.

7. Clean Up All Your High Interest Loans

o Review all loans or advances taken or given and plan to reduce high-interest loans.

o If reducing loans using profits, consider it as advance tax payment; apply interest on loans given and plan for advance tax.

8. Check All Your Statutory Liabilities

- Verify TDS payable, PF/ESI payable, and other statutory liabilities such as local taxes.

- Issue necessary certificates like Form 16A for TDS deducted by you and pay off current liabilities to reduce advances from customers and expenses payable.

9. Calculate GST Turnover

- Ensure GSTR-1 and GSTR-3B are matched with your books of accounts and address any discrepancies before filing the March return.

10. Reconcile GST Ledgers

- Reconcile GST credit ledgers with books of accounts and ensure GSTR-2B matches the input tax credit taken.

- Verify all purchase bills are included in GSTR-2B and reconcile GST TDS deducted by authorities, reflecting the same in GSTR-7A.

11. Make Provisions

- Create provisions for expenses pertaining to the current financial year but due in the next year, such as electricity, audit fees, and salaries.

- Ensure fair presentation of your books and profits by timely provisioning.

12. Check Income Tax TDS & GST TDS Receivable

- Confirm TDS receivable is mentioned in Form 26AS up to the last quarter and request TDS certificates quarterly.

13. Review Your Books of Accounts

- ○ Review your overall books of accounts up to Last Period.

- ○ Perform a comparative analysis with previous years/quarters, check for any unincorporated expenses or bills, and conduct a ratio analysis.

14. Plan for the Future

- ○ Prepare a Standard Operating Procedure (SOP) and a strategy sheet.

- ○ Develop a budget and learn financial terms and discipline for better financial management.

* * *

Chapter Challenge: Test Your Understanding with MCQs

1. **What should be evaluated when reviewing advance tax payments before the March closing?**

   (A) Previous year's tax liabilities
   (B) Current year's turnover
   (C) Profits up to the last quarter
   (D) All of the above

2. **Which investment options are suggested to save tax and secure financial future?**

   (A) Mutual funds
   (B) Fixed deposits
   (C) Life insurance and medical insurance
   (D) Gold

3. **What is essential to avoid additions under Section 43B(h) for non-payment to small and medium enterprises?**

   (A) Timely reconciliation of creditor balances

   (B) Obtaining MSME certificates

   (C) Making payments promptly

   (D) All of the above

4. **When ideally should stock verification be conducted?**

   (A) Annually

   (B) Quarterly

   (C) Biannually

   (D) Monthly

5. **What should be done before filing the March GST return?**

   (A) Verify TDS payable

   (B) Issue Form 16A for TDS deducted

   (C) Reconcile GST credit ledgers

   (D) All of the above

6. **Which statement regarding high-interest loans is true?**

   (A) They should be increased to maximize profits

   (B) They should be ignored until the next financial year

   (C) They should be reviewed and reduced

   (D) They should be extended to other creditors

7. **What should be done regarding statutory liabilities before March closing?**

   (A) Verify TDS payable

   (B) Check GST ITC

   (C) Reconcile Liabilities already paid

   (D) All of the above

8. **What is essential for better financial management as per the provided tips?**

    (A) Regular stock verification

    (B) Reconciliation of GST ledgers

    (C) Creating provisions for future expenses

    (D) Developing a budget and learning financial terms and discipline

9. **What should be reviewed during the overall review of books of accounts?**

    (A) Previous year's turnover

    (B) Comparative analysis with previous years/quarters

    (C) Ratio analysis

    (D) All of the above

10. **Which strategy is suggested for future planning before March closing?**

    (A) Regularizing high-interest loans

    (B) Making provisions for future expenses

    (C) Reconciling GST ledgers

    (D) Preparing a Standard Operating Procedure (SOP) and a strategy sheet

Answers

1.(D),	2.(C),	3.(D),	4.(B),	5.(C),
6.(C),	7.(D),	8.(D),	9.(D)	10.(D)

TECHNOLOGY SOLUTIONS FOR ACCOUNTING- THE FUTURE IS HERE

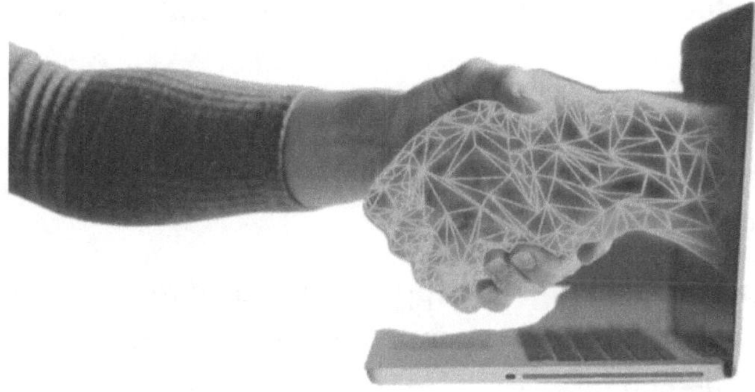

Technology has revolutionized accounting processes for small and medium-sized enterprises (SMEs), offering efficient tools to streamline financial management, enhance accuracy, and improve decision-making. Leveraging technology solutions can empower SMEs to optimize their accounting functions, save time and costs, and ensure compliance with regulatory requirements. In this guide, we explore practical ways to harness technology for accounting in SMEs.

1. Adopt Cloud-Based Accounting Software

Transitioning to cloud-based accounting software offers numerous benefits for SMEs, including accessibility, scalability, and data security. Consider these advantages:

- ○ **Accessibility:** Access financial data anytime, anywhere, and from any device with internet connectivity.

- o **Real-Time Collaboration:** Enable multiple users to work simultaneously on financial records, facilitating teamwork and efficiency.

- o **Automated Updates:** Enjoy automatic software updates and data backups without the need for manual intervention.

Popular cloud-based accounting software options for SMEs include QuickBooks Online, Zoho Books etc.

2. **Automate Routine Accounting Tasks**

   Technology allows SMEs to automate repetitive accounting tasks, reducing manual effort and minimizing errors. Leverage automation for:

   - o **Invoicing and Billing:** Automate the creation and delivery of invoices to customers, reducing payment delays and improving cash flow.

   - o **Expense Tracking:** Use apps or integrated tools to capture and categorize business expenses automatically, ensuring accurate record-keeping.

   - o **Bank Reconciliation:** Automate bank feeds to reconcile transactions with bank statements in real-time, minimizing discrepancies.

3. **Implement Integrated Systems**

   Integrate accounting software with other business systems to streamline data flow and eliminate duplicate data entry. Key integrations include:

   - o **Payment Gateways:** Integrate payment processing solutions to facilitate seamless receipt of customer payments and reconciliation.

   - o **Inventory Management:** Sync accounting software with inventory systems to track stock levels, cost of goods sold (COGS), and inventory valuation.

   - o **Customer Relationship Management (CRM):** Integrate CRM platforms with accounting software to link customer data, sales transactions, and invoicing.

4. **Utilize Mobile Apps for Financial Management**

Mobile apps offer convenience and flexibility for SMEs to manage finances on the go. Explore mobile apps that:

- ○ **Capture Receipts:** Use receipt-scanning apps to capture and digitize paper receipts, facilitating expense management and compliance.

- ○ **Approve Transactions:** Authorize payments, review financial reports, and monitor cash flow using mobile accounting apps.

- ○ **Track Time and Expenses:** Enable remote workers to log billable hours and business expenses directly from their smartphones.

5. **Leverage Data Analytics for Insights**

Harness the power of data analytics to derive actionable insights from financial data and improve decision-making. Implement analytics tools to:

- ○ **Generate Financial Reports:** Automatically generate customized financial reports and dashboards with interactive visualizations.

- ○ **Perform Trend Analysis:** Identify patterns, trends, and anomalies in financial data to forecast future performance and mitigate risks.

- ○ Optimize Budgeting and Forecasting: Use predictive analytics to enhance accuracy in budgeting and financial forecasting processes.

6. **Enhance Security Measures**

Prioritize data security to protect sensitive financial information from unauthorized access or cyber threats. Implement robust security measures such as:

- ○ **Two-Factor Authentication (2FA):** Require two-step verification for accessing accounting software and financial data.

- ○ **Data Encryption:** Encrypt financial data both in transit and at rest to safeguard confidentiality and integrity.

- o **Regular Updates:** Keep accounting software and security systems up to date with the latest patches and security enhancements.

7. **Engage with Virtual CFO Services**
   Consider leveraging virtual Chief Financial Officer (CFO) services for strategic financial guidance and management. Virtual CFOs offer expertise in:

   - o **Financial Planning:** Develop comprehensive financial strategies aligned with business goals and market trends.

   - o **Risk Management:** Identify and mitigate financial risks through proactive analysis and contingency planning.

   - o **Investment Advisory:** Provide insights into capital allocation, investment opportunities, and funding strategies.

8. **Stay Compliant with Regulatory Requirements**
   Use technology to ensure compliance with regulatory standards and financial reporting obligations. Leverage features such as:

   - o **Automatic Tax Calculations:** Enable automated tax calculations and compliance checks within accounting software.

   - o **Audit Trails:** Maintain detailed audit trails and transaction histories for regulatory audits and compliance reviews.

   - o **Regulatory Updates:** Receive real-time alerts and notifications about changes in tax laws, accounting standards, and regulatory frameworks affecting SMEs.

9. **Invest in Employee Training**
   Empower employees with training on accounting software and technology solutions to maximize their productivity and proficiency. Provide resources and support for:

   - o **Software Training:** Conduct workshops or online tutorials to familiarize employees with accounting software features and functionalities.

- ○ **Continuous Learning:** Encourage ongoing learning and skill development to keep pace with technological advancements in financial management.

10. Regularly Evaluate and Optimize Technology Solutions

Continuously assess the effectiveness of technology solutions and make adjustments as needed to optimize accounting processes. Regularly evaluate:

- ○ **Performance Metrics:** Monitor key performance indicators (KPIs) related to financial management efficiency, accuracy, and compliance.

- ○ **User Feedback:** Solicit feedback from accounting teams and stakeholders to identify areas for improvement and implement enhancements.

- ○ **Technology Trends:** Stay informed about emerging technologies and innovations in accounting software to leverage new capabilities and stay competitive.

By embracing technology solutions tailored for accounting, SMEs can streamline financial operations, enhance decision-making, and drive sustainable growth. Integrating automation, data analytics, and mobile capabilities into accounting practices empowers SMEs to navigate challenges, capitalize on opportunities, and thrive in today's digital economy.

* * *

Chapter Challenge: Test Your Understanding with MCQs

1. **Which of the following is NOT a benefit of transitioning to cloud-based accounting software for SMEs?**

   (A) Improved accessibility

   (B) Enhanced data security

   (C) Manual software updates

   (D) Real-time collaboration

2. **What is one task that can be automated using technology solutions in accounting for SMEs?**

   (A) Manual bank reconciliation

   (B) Automated tax calculations

   (C) Continuous user feedback

   (D) Software training workshops

3. **Which integration is recommended to streamline data flow and eliminate duplicate data entry in accounting for SMEs?**

   (A) Integration with inventory management systems

   (B) Integration with email marketing software

   (C) Integration with social media platforms

   (D) Integration with project management tools

4. **How can mobile apps contribute to financial management for SMEs?**

   (A) Monitoring cash flow via email notifications

   (B) Manual transaction approval

   (C) Tracking time and expenses only on desktops

   (D) Capturing and digitizing paper receipts

5. **Which security measure is essential for protecting sensitive financial information in accounting for SMEs?**

   (A) Data encryption

   (B) Public sharing of financial reports

   (C) Using outdated security systems

   (D) Single-step verification

Answers

1.(C),   2.(A),   3.(A),   4.(D),   5.(A)

GLOSSARY - ACCOUNTING DEFINITIONS

1. **Accrual Accounting**: Recognizing revenues and expenses when they are earned or incurred rather than when cash is exchanged.

2. **Accounts Payable**: Money owed by a business to its creditors for goods or services received but not yet paid for.

3. **Accounts Receivable**: Money owed to a business by its customers for goods or services provided on credit.

4. **Accumulated Depreciation**: Total depreciation expense accumulated over the life of an asset, reducing its book value.

5. **Amortization**: Similar to depreciation but applicable to intangible assets like patents or trademarks, expensing their cost over their useful life.

6. **Assets**: Resources owned by a business that have future economic value, such as cash, inventory, equipment, or property.

7. **Assessment Year:** The year following the financial year in which income is assessed for taxation purposes.

8. **Audit**: Independent examination of financial statements to ensure accuracy and compliance with regulations.

9. **Balance Sheet**: A financial statement summarizing a company's assets, liabilities, and equity at a specific point in time.

10. **Book Value**: The value of an asset or liability as recorded on the balance sheet, often representing its cost less accumulated depreciation.

11. **Bookkeeping**: Recording financial transactions and maintaining financial records systematically.

12. **Bottom Line:** Represents the net income or profit after accounting for all expenses and taxes, reflecting the overall financial performance of the company

13. **Capital**: Assets or funds used to generate revenue or the owner's stake in a business.

14. **Capital Adequacy Ratio**: Indicates a bank's financial stability by comparing its capital to risk-weighted assets.

15. **Cash Basis Accounting**: Recording revenues and expenses only when cash is exchanged, not when they are earned or incurred.

16. **Cash Equivalents**: Short-term, highly liquid investments easily convertible to cash.

17. **Cash Flow**: Movement of cash into and out of a business during a specific period.

18. **Chart of Accounts**: Master list of accounts used in a company's general ledger to categorize transactions.

19. **Consolidated Financial Statements**: Combined financial statements of a parent company and its subsidiaries.

20. **Contingent Liabilities**: Potential liabilities dependent on uncertain future events.

21. **Cost of Goods Sold (COGS)**: Direct costs incurred in producing goods or services sold by a company.

22. **Credit**: Accounting entry that increases liabilities or decreases assets.

23. **Debt Service Coverage Ratio**: Measures a company's ability to cover debt payments with its operating income.

24. **Debt-to-Equity Ratio**: Total debt divided by shareholders' equity, indicating financial leverage.

25. **Deferred Revenue**: Payment received in advance for goods or services to be provided in the future.

26. **Deferred Revenue Expenditure:** Expenditure incurred in one financial year but its benefit extends beyond that year, hence is written off over a period of time.

27. **Depreciation**: Allocation of the cost of a tangible asset over its useful life.

28. **Dividend Payout Ratio**: Proportion of earnings paid out to shareholders as dividends.

29. **Dividend Yield**: Annual dividends per share divided by share price, showing return to shareholders.

30. **Dividends**: Payments made to shareholders as a distribution of company profits.

31. **Double-Entry Bookkeeping**: Accounting system recording transactions as debits and credits to maintain balance.

32. **EBIT (Earnings Before Interest and Taxes)**: Operating profit before deducting interest and taxes.

33. **EBITDA (Earnings Before Interest, Taxes, Depreciation, and Amortization)**: Measure of operating performance.

34. **EBITDA Margin**: EBITDA divided by revenue, indicating operating profitability excluding non-operating factors.

35. **EBIT Interest Coverage Ratio**: Measures a company's ability to cover interest expenses with operating income.

36. **EBIT Margin**: EBIT divided by revenue, showing operating profitability as a percentage.

37. **EBT (Earnings Before Tax)**: Income before tax expenses are deducted.

38. **Equity**: Ownership value in a business, calculated as assets minus liabilities.

39. **Expenses**: Costs incurred to generate revenue during a specific period.

40. **Fair Value**: The price at which an asset could be exchanged or a liability settled in an orderly transaction.

41. **Financial Forecast**: Prediction of future financial outcomes based on past performance and market trends.

42. **Financial Leverage**: Use of debt to increase potential return on equity.

43. **Financial Modeling**: Creating mathematical representations of financial situations or assets.

44. **Financial Ratios**: Quantitative indicators used to assess a company's financial health and performance.

45. **Financial Statements Footnotes**: Supplementary notes providing additional details to the financial statements.

46. **Financial Year:** A 12-month period used for financial reporting and tax purposes by businesses and governments.

47. **Fixed Cost**: Expense that remains constant regardless of business activity.

48. **Free Cash Flow**: Operating cash flow minus capital expenditures, representing cash available for distribution.

49. **General Ledger**: Master record of all financial transactions in a company.

50. **Gearing Ratio**: Compares a company's debt to its equity, assessing financial risk.

51. **Going Concern**: Assumption that a company will continue its operations for the foreseeable future.

52. **Goodwill**: Intangible asset representing the premium paid for acquiring another company above its book value.

53. **Gross Profit**: Revenue minus the cost of goods sold, representing profitability from sales.

54. **Hedging**: Using financial instruments to reduce or offset the risk of adverse price movements in assets or liabilities.

55. **Income Statement**: Financial statement detailing revenues, expenses, and net income over a period.

56. **Impairment**: Reduction in the value of an asset below its carrying amount on the balance sheet.

57. **Income Statement**: Financial statement detailing revenues, expenses, and net income over a period.

58. **Intrinsic Value**: True value of a company's stock based on its fundamentals.

59. **Internal Controls**: Policies and procedures designed to safeguard assets and ensure accurate financial reporting.

60. **Intangible Assets**: Non-physical assets with long-term value, such as patents, trademarks, or goodwill.

61. **Interim Financial Statements**: Financial reports issued between annual reporting periods.

62. **Inventory**: Goods held for sale or raw materials used in production.

63. **Inventory Turnover**: How many times inventory is sold and replaced in a period, showing efficiency.

64. **Leverage Ratio**: Measures the proportion of debt in a company's capital structure.

65. **Liability**: Financial obligation or debt owed by a company.

66. **Liquidity**: Ease of converting assets into cash.

67. **Liquidity Ratio**: Measures a company's ability to meet short-term obligations.

68. **Market Capitalization**: Total value of a company's outstanding shares calculated as share price times outstanding shares.

69. **Market Value**: Current value of an asset based on market conditions and demand.

70. **Material Weakness**: Significant deficiency in internal controls that could result in financial misstatement.

71. **Materiality**: Significance of an item or event in relation to financial statements and decision-making.

72. **Net Income**: Total revenue minus total expenses, also known as profit or earnings.

73. **Non-operating Income/Expenses**: Income or expenses not directly related to core business activities.

74. **Operating Cash Flow**: Cash generated from core business operations.

75. **Operating Cash Flow Ratio**: Compares cash generated from operations to current liabilities.

76. **Operating Cycle**: Time required for a company to purchase, produce, and sell inventory, and collect cash.

77. **Operating Expenses**: Costs incurred from normal business operations, excluding cost of goods sold.

78. **Operating Income**: Gross profit minus operating expenses, showing profit from core business activities.

79. **Operating Leverage**: Use of fixed costs to magnify changes in operating income.

80. **Overhead**: Operating expenses not directly tied to production or services.

81. **Payables Turnover Ratio**: Measures how quickly a company pays its suppliers.

82. **Payroll**: Accounting for employee compensation and benefits.

83. **Present Value**: Adjusting future cash flows to their current value.

84. **Price-to-Book (P/B) Ratio**: Compares a company's market value to its book value per share.

85. **Price-to-Earnings (P/E) Ratio**: Share price divided by earnings per share, indicating valuation relative to earnings.

86. **Profitability Ratio**: Indicates a company's ability to generate profit relative to revenue or assets.

87. **Receivables Turnover Ratio**: Measures how efficiently a company collects accounts receivable.

88. **Receipt**: Written record of a financial transaction.

89. **Reserves**: Funds set aside for specific purposes, such as contingencies or future expenses.

90. **Return on Assets (ROA)**: Net income divided by average total assets, indicating efficiency in asset utilization.

91. **Return on Equity (ROE)**: Net income divided by average shareholders' equity, showing profitability relative to equity.

92. **Return on Investment (ROI)**: Profitability measure showing return on an investment relative to its cost.

93. **Risk Management**: Identifying, assessing, and managing risks to minimize negative impacts on objectives.

94. **Segment Reporting**: Reporting of financial data for different operating segments of a company.

95. **Shareholders' Equity**: Residual interest in assets after deducting liabilities.

96. **Solvency Ratio**: Measures a company's ability to meet long-term obligations.

97. **Tangible Assets**: Physical assets with a finite useful life, such as property, equipment, or inventory.

98. **Tax Expense**: Total amount of taxes payable by a company based on its earnings and applicable tax laws.

99. **Top Line:** Refers to a company's total revenue or sales generated from its core business operations.

100. **Trial Balance**: Report of all general ledger account balances at a specific time.

101. **Variable Cost**: Expenses that change with business activity or sales volume.

102. **Weighted Average Cost of Capital (WACC)**: Weighted average of a company's cost of debt and equity financing.

103. **Working Capital**: Current assets minus current liabilities, reflecting operational liquidity.

104. **Working Capital Management**: Strategies to optimize the use of current assets and liabilities.